JACKIE ROBINSON

Books by Manfred Weidhorn

NAPOLEON

ROBERT E. LEE

JACKIE ROBINSON

JACKIE
ROBINSON

by
MANFRED WEIDHORN

ATHENEUM   1993   NEW YORK
Maxwell Macmillan Canada
Toronto
Maxwell Macmillan International
New York   Oxford   Singapore   Sydney

Copyright © 1993 by Manfred Weidhorn

Atheneum
Macmillan Publishing Company
866 Third Avenue
New York, NY 10022

Maxwell Macmillan Canada, Inc.
1200 Eglinton Avenue East
Suite 200
Don Mills, Ontario M3C 3N1

Macmillan Publishing Company is part of
the Maxwell Communication Group of Companies.

First edition

Printed in the United States of America

92721   10 9 8 7 6 5 4 3 2 1

The text of this book is set in Bodoni.

Library of Congress Cataloging-in-Publication Data

Weidhorn, Manfred, 1931–
Jackie Robinson / by Manfred Weidhorn.—1st ed.
p.   cm.
Includes bibliographical references (p. 199).
Summary: A biography of the Afro-American who fought racial
injustice both during and after his celebrated baseball career.
ISBN 0–689–31644–5
1. Robinson, Jackie, 1919–1972—Juvenile literature.   2. Baseball
players—United States—Biography—Juvenile literature.
[1. Robinson, Jackie, 1919–1972.   2. Baseball players.   3. Afro-
Americans—Biography.]   I. Title.
GV865.R6W45   1993
796.357'092—dc20
[B]   92–15248

To my family

CONTENTS

Contents

1

AN EXPERIMENT IN BASEBALL
(April 15, 1947)

April 15, 1947, was a cloudy, chilly spring day in Brooklyn, New York. For most people in that famous "borough of churches" it was just another workday. They had their breakfast, traveled to their job or store, and, eight or ten hours later, returned home for dinner. For those who were baseball fans, however, something special was in the air. It was opening day for the home-town major league baseball team, the Dodgers.

If baseball is America's national sport, in Brooklyn in those days it was more like a religion. For many people, especially children and teenagers, opening day was just about the most important event on the calendar. It meant that the long winter of waiting was over. It meant that the endless hours of cold weather bull sessions would finally be replaced by those daily battle-field news bulletins known as baseball scores. It meant the beginning of a half year of daily box scores, league standings, pennant races, chewing gum baseball cards, and the heroic achievements of favorite ballplayers.

It meant many afternoons spent in that small, cozy ballpark—Ebbets Field—which was in some ways the living room of Brooklyn. And, of course, opening day could eventually mean—if only for once things worked out right—a chance at a World Series. Autumn would bring the sad return to school, but that disaster was made up for by the thought that the Brooklyn Dodgers could be world champions.

In the spring of 1947, such an outcome was a possibility. The Dodgers, one of the most colorful teams in baseball even while doing poorly in the 1920s and 1930s, had made it to the World Series in 1941. During the years of World War II, 1942–1945, the Dodgers drifted again. But in 1946, they had caught fire.

They played so well that they found themselves in first place. Unfortunately, they were not alone; they shared it with the St. Louis Cardinals. A three-game play-off series was to decide the league championship. Imagine having fought hard in 154 games during five and a half long months only to have everything decided by a single game! It was like tossing a coin to see who got to play in the World Series.

The Dodgers lost that one. A heartbroken Brooklyn tried to console itself with the slogan that had taken hold during the war years: "Wait till next year!" Mixing disappointment, pain and defiance, wishful thinking, and hoped-for revenge, this slogan for once seemed to mean something.

The Dodgers had been one game away from the World Series. There were good reasons to think that the 1947 Dodgers would be as good as the previous year's team. They had Dixie Walker, "the People's Choice," a .300 hitter and former batting champion; Pee Wee Reese, perhaps the best fielding and hitting shortstop around; Eddie Stanky, the scrappy little second baseman, who specialized in getting on base one way or another; and Pistol Pete Reiser, once one of the most promising rookie outfielders in years and still a classy player when he did not crash into outfield walls. And there was also a fine pitching staff consisting of Hugh Casey, Hal Gregg, Kirby Higbe, and others. Opening day was looked forward to with even more excitement than in the past.

Then two dramatic developments late in spring training made this opening day different from all others. One involved the manager of the team, and the other a rookie player.

Leo Durocher, the manager of the Dodgers, had long been one of the most exciting and controversial men in baseball. He was loud, stormy, hard driving. After ball games he liked to step out on the town, but in the ballpark he was all business. Though ruthless with his players, he knew how to get the best out of them.

Everything he did was for the good of the team. The Brooklyn fans especially loved it when he came out of the dugout to scream at the umpire if he thought a wrong call had been made. Veins bulging out on his neck, eyes glaring, teeth and chin stuck in the umpires' faces, hands motioning wildly, jaw working away, he put on quite a show. People thought they could hear his voice all over the ballpark. He made yelling at umpires as great an art form as hitting a home run or stealing home. Surely "Leo the Lip" had played no small role in bringing the Dodgers back to life in 1946. Surely he would lead them into an even more successful charge at the pennant this time.

Suddenly, on the eve of the baseball season, something shocking and unexpected happened. A. B. "Happy" Chandler, the commissioner of baseball, suspended Durocher for a whole year on the charge of hanging around with gamblers.

True, Durocher *did* have this weakness, and he had been warned before about the company he kept. On the other hand, he was not the only one in baseball guilty of this lapse. The suddenness of the suspension, the apparent unfairness with which it was made, and the terrible timing of having it take place just as the season was about to begin—all this threatened to disrupt the plans and preparations of the Dodgers.

What made the suspension even more awkward was that it came on the eve of one of the greatest developments in the history of organized baseball: the introduction of a black man as a major league player.

Nowadays, in the closing years of the twentieth century, with African Americans playing such an impressive role in nearly all professional sports, it may be difficult to believe that during the first half century of its history, modern major league baseball had no black players in it at all.

The general manager of the Brooklyn Dodgers, Branch Rickey, had decided to break that tradition. When he thought that he had at last found his candidate, Rickey gave him careful instructions on how to handle the human, personal side of the experiment. Then he sent him off for the 1946 season to the Montreal Royals.

During his season in Montreal, as well as in the championship play-offs at the end of the season, this man performed better than expected. So, the next year he was brought up to the Dodgers, just a few days before the season began. That is what made April 15, 1947, extra special. That day was to be a landmark in the history of the United States as well as of baseball.

It would have been a difficult day under any circumstances, but unexpected events made it much more so. Leo Durocher was, like Rickey, a man who believed that what mattered was not the skin color of a player but his skill on the baseball diamond. Winning was far more important than color prejudice. He therefore had eagerly participated in the preparation of the new player for the team and the team for the player. To have Durocher taken away just hours before the beginning of the season was a first-class disaster.

As if that was not bad enough, things were made worse by the fact that the team proved more resistant to change than had been expected. Reporters and team officials heard unsettling rumors. And not only about the Dodgers. Petitions were said to be circulating on some teams. Players were reportedly being pressured to sign—or not sign. It was said some baseball players would refuse to play in any game in which a black man participated.

Up in the broadcasting booth was the great Red

Barber, the "voice of Brooklyn," the Dodgers announcer with the southern drawl, whom fans loved. Born in Mississippi and raised in Florida, he too had toyed with the idea of walking out on his job.

It looked like everything was coming apart at once. To top off all this turmoil in those mid-April days, there was no general on the battlefield, no field manager to replace Durocher. Just when leadership was needed, uncertainty was the order of the day. What man would be crazy enough to want to take over this particular baseball team at the last minute of spring training and walk into such a tension-ridden situation? There might be mutinies in the clubhouses and maybe even riots in the streets.

It would be hard to imagine the pressures on the individual at the center of all this attention on that day. Baseball players differ from most people because, unlike doctors, lawyers, and accountants, they perform in front of tens of thousands of spectators. They are judged at once. They get to hear very clearly from the fans whether they are doing well or not. That is a difficult enough burden for any player, especially for a rookie, but the first black man carried a weight that was magnified tenfold, or a hundredfold.

It would be a rare person, black or white, who could survive in the pressure cooker Ebbets Field had become on that spring day of 1947. Now, as the visiting team pitcher prepared to pitch to the second batter in the home half of the first inning of the opening day game, a good portion of America hunched forward in suspense. Had Rickey found the right person? Would the experiment work? It had worked in Montreal, but that was a minor league and another country, whereas this was "the show," the big time, the majors, the real test in the United States.

Jack Roosevelt Robinson stepped up to the plate. With him, 20 million Americans took their first turn at bat in modern major league baseball.

2

FROM GEORGIA TO CALIFORNIA
(1919-1933)

Jack Roosevelt Robinson was born on January 31, 1919, in a small farmhouse near Cairo, Georgia. Though he would some day capture newspaper headlines all across America, little about this birth attracted anyone's attention. The man who was to arouse the pride and the fear, the respect and the loathing, of millions of Americans could not have been born with a more unpromising beginning.

Jackie was born with black skin. That seemingly unimportant fact shaped his life. Born black into a white world, he—as he said near the end of his life—never had it made.

Most black people had first come to America hundreds of years before, not as explorers, immigrants, or tourists, but as slaves on ships from Africa. Here they lived lives of extreme misery. Eventually a civil war erupted over the existence of this barbaric institution. The antislavery North triumphed over the slaveholding South. The slaves were freed at last in the 1860s.

What occurred in the South after the Civil War was the instituting of a sort of secondhand, or invisible, slavery. The races were kept apart—segregated—by state laws. White people did not want to have to meet on an equal basis with individuals from an allegedly inferior race. Blacks were therefore not allowed into the regular public schools and colleges. They were not allowed alongside whites in restaurants, churches, swimming pools, parks and playgrounds, even in rest rooms or at drinking fountains. Though blacks were supposed to have their own facilities, under the slogan of "separate but equal," in fact whatever was available to them was vastly inferior. As a result, blacks were foreigners in their own country. They were citizens of a nation that offered equal opportunity to everyone— as long as he or she was white. This was the world Jackie Robinson was born into.

His ancestors had been slaves. His maternal grandfather was, like many southern blacks, a sharecropper on a cotton plantation. A sharecropper lived on a white man's land and paid his rent by giving, instead of cash, a major portion of his crops to the landowner. The grandfather tended the crops and harvested them but had no rights of possession.

Jackie's mother, Mallie McGriff, in 1909 had married Jerry Robinson, a sharecropper like her father. Pay was very low, favors were few. The couple soon began having children. Theirs was a life of poverty and hardship.

Mallie early on showed her special grit and determination. At her prompting, Jerry went to the plantation owner and asked for a better deal. Thus he became a "half cropper," someone getting half the profits of whatever he grew. A hard worker, Jerry managed to achieve a certain amount of prosperity.

As it turned out, doing well ruined everything. Able now to wear better clothes and to have a little extra spending money, Jerry turned to the fast life in town. By the time Jackie was born, there were already four other children in the family, and Jerry was not around much.

A few months later, Jerry left his family forever, running off to Florida with someone else's wife. Not only was Mallie abandoned with five children to take care of, but the plantation owner blamed her for Jerry's leaving. He forced her out of the house into a miserable shack. She got work as a housemaid, and the children had to fend for themselves.

Little Jackie was born at the low point of his mother's life. He started out in a broken home, deep in poverty, without a father, surrounded by prejudice and hatred, and with a mother who had to spend the day working elsewhere. If Jackie was to rise above the life he was born into, he would have a lot of mountains to climb.

Many blacks were leaving the South during these years. One of them was Burton, Mallie's brother. He had been in the army during World War I and had stayed in California, where he had been stationed, after his discharge. He did quite well for himself as a self-taught landscape artist and gardener, and now he encouraged his sister to join him.

So in May 1920 Mallie sold her furniture and clothing to the neighbors and used the money for train fare to California. The family settled in Pasadena, a suburb of Los Angeles, where many movie stars lived. Within a few days Mallie found a job washing and ironing. With the money from this work, with money from the local welfare agency, with gifts from friendly neighbors, with what the children chipped in whenever they earned something, and with lots of religious faith, Mallie held her family together.

The children saw little of their mother. She was gone before they were up, and they were in bed by the time she returned. Sometimes when she brought home leftovers from a dinner party, they had a decent meal. The money was small, the work was hard, the jobs changed, and a lot of mouths had to be fed, but she was determined to put the kids through school. As Jackie grew up, he became more aware of his mother's many burdens and vowed that some day he would relieve her of them.

Mallie was soon able to rent a house at the border between the black and white parts of town. Though California was not in the South, racial prejudice in America knows no boundaries. For a long time she and her children were to encounter harassment and bigotry. Jackie grew up hearing the word "nigger" thrown at him with clenched teeth. One neighbor called the police when black kids so much as came out to play. There was a cross-burning incident and a petition to try to force the Robinson family to move out.

Jackie was proud of his mother, who would not

allow the white neighbors to drive her away or frighten her or mistreat her kids. From her he learned to stand up for his rights. He learned to respect himself, demand respect from others, and never back down.

Jackie was always on the go; he ran rather than walked. His favorite activity was hitting with a stick a rag ball his mother had made for him. Eventually he joined his brothers and sisters in getting the typical odd jobs of kids—delivering newspapers or groceries, mowing grass, running errands, shining shoes, selling hot dogs.

Jackie preferred playing ball to studying. He became very good at it, and when sides were chosen up for sandlot softball games, he was allowed to share in the lunches of the kids on the team he played with. Sometimes that might be the only food he had that day. Or he was given a dollar, which he would then turn over dutifully to his mother. That was, in a way, his entry into professional sports.

Jackie discovered at an early age that sports was one area where he could compete freely with whites. He played soccer on his fourth-grade team. He played baseball in his early teens against men's teams. Because he was a fine athlete, he was treated by the white kids as an equal and as a friend, both in primary and high school. Winning in sports, he remarked later, took some of the sting out of being an outsider.

His friendships were not with whites only. He joined a local gang of black, Japanese, and Mexican kids. The Pepper Street Gang was an informal sports club, not a violent street gang. They played all sorts of games, and Jackie stood out in all of them. To earn money they hunted for lost golf balls. These they would sell back to the owners on the nearby golf courses. Jackie's good eyes enabled him to find the most balls.

It was hard for Jackie to find a reason to excel at school. Those black kids he knew who studied hard and got good grades ended up as bellhops, porters, and taxi drivers. On the other hand, through high school sports, Jackie met lots of people of all races, traveled quite a bit in southern California and elsewhere, and learned a few things about life. One of the things he learned was that segregation and bigotry were not so solid in sports when people had a strong desire to win.

The Pepper Street Gang members were no angels. Sometimes they stole things from stores, especially from fruit stands. At other times they would throw dirt at passing cars or go swimming illegally in the reservoir. This last activity brought them into several run-ins with the police, who were horrified at the thought of a bunch of "nigger kids" swimming in the city's drinking water.

Jackie might well have been on the way to turning into a juvenile delinquent, but he was saved by his athletic ability and by a local minister, Karl Downs. The minister got the young people involved in social and sports activities at the church. In fact, Jackie was so influenced by the minister that he later became a

Sunday school teacher. The minister watched Jackie play football on Saturday and made sure Jackie taught Sunday school the next morning. Those Saturday and Sunday activities were his first small steps out of poverty and aimlessness.

3

AN ATHLETE FOR ALL SEASONS
(1933-1941)

Jackie grew up during the Great Depression. He was a teenager in the 1930s, when one out of every four Americans was out of work. For blacks, the picture was even grimmer. Few jobs and hardly any professions were available to them. Those who spent most of their time in the gym or the backyard, or on the playing field, did it not because blacks are naturally better at sports than at brain work but because sports were their way out of poverty. Some blacks now were starting to make it in college football and in professional boxing. The great role model here was Joe Louis, the heavyweight boxer.

So when Jackie started attending Washington Junior High School in 1933, his main interest was sports. He was good at them, and he had an example in his own brother Mack. Six years older, Mack was so good a track-and-field man that he would go on to win a silver medal at the 1936 Berlin Olympics, finishing second behind the great black runner Jesse Owens in the 200-meter dash.

Jackie's athletic abilities sprouted in all directions. Whatever sport he took up, he became the best at it. He was as good in individual sports—handball, badminton, tennis—as in team sports. As soon as he learned to play Ping-Pong, he won the city championship and, for the first time, got his name in the newspaper. The Washington school teams won because he was on them.

He next went to Muir Technical High School, where his athletic achievements piled up. Soon he was singled out as the player to beat, and the strategy of the opposing teams was "Stop Robinson!" He enjoyed this reputation.

Sometimes he seemed hotheaded and cocky to schoolmates and coaches. Some blacks had learned from years of second-class citizenship to hold their rage and to turn the other cheek. Jackie was not one of that sort.

His mother had instilled pride, determination, and self-respect in her children. His brother Mack was an example. Mack had a heart condition; he was warned by doctors not to continue in sports. Yet he ignored them and made it to the Olympics. Like mother and brother, Jackie was a fighter. The self-assertiveness might have made him seem arrogant, but it helped lead the teams he played on to triumph on the field.

Curiously, Jackie put on a poor show during practice sessions. It was as if, consciously or not, he were pacing himself, holding the best part of himself in reserve for the game, when everything was on the line; as if practice were only a game and the game itself were something grimly serious. He needed the stimulus of competition and the goal of victory.

To some teammates, opponents, and bystanders, such intensity was out of place in mere sports. But this seriousness would bring out the best in him in the most challenging and difficult situations. It made him a clutch hitter. And it would make him the man for the great breakthrough in baseball. His future success was not just a matter of unique athletic skill but also of character. A better ballplayer than he might have wilted under conditions in which he thrived.

After graduating from high school in 1937, Jackie entered Pasadena Junior College. Many famous athletes and actors have gone there. At first he was known mainly as the younger brother of Mack Robinson, the Olympics runner. Then he established his own identity. After a slow start because of a broken ankle, he became a star quarterback on the football team. The team lost every game when he was out with the injury and won every game when he returned. In game after game, Jackie made breathtaking runs. Winning eleven straight games, Pasadena became the junior college champions and went to the play-offs at the Rose Bowl. In the game at the Rose Bowl, Jackie made a great interception and touchdown run that helped the team to victory.

He next turned to basketball. He became the highest scorer on a team that was one of the best in the school's history. Averaging 19 points a game, he again led Pasadena to a California junior college championship. He was elected to an all-state team. Always his aggressive personality accompanied his outstanding abilities. In one game, Jackie found himself fouled by an opposing player one time too many. He lost his temper and a brawl ensued.

After football in the fall and basketball in the winter, Jackie joined the track and the baseball teams in the spring. He was an outstanding hitter and base stealer, as well as an All–Southern California Junior College shortstop.

Participating in two sports at the same time was not easy. Sure enough, one day there was a conflict between a track meet and a baseball game. As neither coach was willing to sacrifice him for the sake of the rival sport, special arrangements had to be made so that Jackie could manage to participate in both events.

He was given permission to compete in the track meet in the morning, and then was rushed by car to the baseball game in the afternoon at another field. As if that were not splendid enough, he managed in the morning to set a new college record for the broad jump—breaking the world record set by his own brother Mack! Then in the afternoon baseball game, he helped the Pasadena team win the league championship. He was observed and idolized by a student at a neighboring school, future Dodger teammate and Hall of Famer Duke Snider.

Jackie won the southern California baseball batting championship with a .417 average. He stole 25 bases in 24 games. One sportswriter called him the greatest base runner ever on a junior college team. Naturally he was voted the Most Valuable Player of the Southern California Junior College League. In March 1938, he played in an exhibition game against the major league Chicago White Sox. He got two hits and made three fine plays in the field. The White Sox manager was awed. He said that no one in the American League was that good and that if only Jackie were white he would have been signed up right away for $50,000 (a big sum in those days).

In the fall of 1938, Jackie put together a sensational season on the Pasadena football team. He was a "triple threat": He could run, pass, and kick. As the quarterback, he was the team leader, brains, and spark plug. In one game he scored three touchdowns by his passing and three more by running.

Even then he showed that personal success did not blind him to the plight of fellow blacks. Some black teammates were being picked on by southerners on the team. Aware that he was necessary to the team, Jackie told the coach that he would transfer to a rival college if the harassment did not stop. The coach quickly took the necessary actions. Jackie learned that, when facing bigotry, you could get justice if you kept your cool and used your strong card. For an athlete, the strong card is the ability to win.

Jackie's athletic record was amazing. He was the NCAA champion in the national junior college broad jump competition. He won the Pacific Coast intercollegiate golf championship. He reached the semifinals of the national Negro tennis tournament. Recruiters from many big, faraway colleges offered scholarships and other inducements to Jackie. He chose to go to UCLA so that he could be close to his mother and close to the nearby job market.

In the fall of 1939, his first year at UCLA, he early on became involved in a racial incident. He was in a car with friends when it was bumped from behind by a white driver. An argument developed, and the ever-aggressive Jackie was arraigned and booked on suspicion of robbery. Because bond money was posted by the Pasadena baseball coach, he did not have to go to jail. Told by school officials that everything was settled, Jackie skipped a court appearance, only to find out that he had forfeited the bond. The charge was finally dropped, but the money was not refunded.

Because of incidents like these, Jackie had a reputation of being difficult. But he had a far greater reputation as one of the finest athletes in the school's history. He participated in football, basketball, baseball, and track. He was an extraordinary running back in football and a star forward in basketball, leading the league in scoring. He won the Pacific Coast League and then the national collegiate championship in the broad jump.

In the football season that fall, Jackie was the star in several key games. He outdid himself in a game against a Stanford team that had a legendary backfield. He intercepted a pass, made a great run for a touchdown, and then kicked successfully for the extra point. Almost single-handedly he stopped the Stanford powerhouse. The Stanford coach called Jackie "the greatest backfield runner" he had ever seen, someone even greater than the renowned Red Grange. He ended the season as the best runner in college football, averaging twelve yards per attempt. He had the unusually high average of twenty-one yards per punt return. Under his leadership, the UCLA team almost made it to the Rose Bowl that year.

As usual, winter saw him switch to basketball. For two years in a row he led the Southern Pacific Basketball Conference in scoring. One of the California coaches called him the best basketball player in America. In a crucial game against the archrival USC team, he scored more than half of his team's winning thirty-five points.

In 1940 he was invited to the annual football game pitting the college all-stars against the professional Chicago Bears. In Chicago, surrounded by the outstanding college football players of the year from all over the country, he held his own. Though the collegians were smashed by the pros, Jackie's tremendous catch scored one of the two touchdowns made by his team.

During this school year, Jackie, a senior now and the most important athlete on campus, met pretty Rachel Isum. She was a freshman honor student majoring in nursing. She came from a middle-class family, but because of illness in the family she had to work her way through college. Jackie was merely polite to her, and she was put off by his arrogant appearance, by the way he stood with hands on hips in the football backfield.

She quickly discovered that the arrogance was partly a cover for deep shyness. Though famous, Jackie was difficult to approach socially. He was unsure of himself around women and had seldom gone out with them. His poverty and his dark skin made him feel out of place among the middle-class black women at college, who often preferred lighter skinned and more affluent black men.

A sensitive, intelligent woman, Rachel was able to find the warm person hidden behind that cold exterior. She knew how to break through the wall of isolation and make him feel at ease. Each found conversation with the other to be exciting. He liked her because she was not a glamour queen but an intelligent woman who had her own goals in life. She liked him because he was not only an athlete but a proud, sensitive man who was ready to speak out against acts of prejudice and injustice. Each admired the individualism and independence of the other.

They saw a lot of each other, at first between classes and at the school parking lot. Then they dated sometimes, and he visited her house, without, however, impressing her father. Soon, he was in love with her. But theirs was to be a long and difficult courtship.

Though his mother wanted him to be a doctor or a lawyer, Jackie was still not the studying type. He majored in physical education and neglected academic studies. Early in 1941, a few months before graduation, Jackie surprised everyone with the abrupt decision to quit college. Money was needed at home, and a job had presented itself. He had come to realize that as good as he was, he had no future in professional sports. Like other black athletes, he led a curious double life. On the field, he was a star cheered by thousands. Once he stepped out of the clubhouse, he was a nobody. No one ever said to him as was said to many a promising young white athlete, "You'll go far someday!" What he, like other outstanding blacks, heard instead was, "Too bad you're not white!"

If education did not prepare a black man for a career, neither did athletic achievement. Blacks were becoming accepted as members of college sports teams, but no matter how great their achievement on the field, as soon as they were graduated, they became second-class citizens again, good only for menial, manual jobs. There were no blacks in professional football, basketball, or baseball. All the doors that had opened for Jackie in high school and college would slam shut on the day of graduation. He would have a roomful of trophies and no job.

With no future in college or in athletics, the best he could hope for was to become a coach or athletic director at a black college or high school. Therefore he seized the chance to work at a camp for poor and orphaned children run by the federal government's National Youth Administration (NYA). If he did well there, he might become athletic director of the next camp to be opened. His mother and Rachel urged him to remain in school for the few months left and get the college degree, but Jackie feared that if he passed up this job in order to graduate, another opportunity might not come along.

Jackie left UCLA in a blaze of articles praising him to the skies as an all-around athlete. He was the first person in the history of UCLA to win four varsity letters for sports in one year. One columnist, calling him "the UCLA Phenomenon" and "the greatest colored athlete of all time," compared Jackie with such special black athletes as Jesse Owens, Paul Robeson, Jack Johnson, and Joe Louis. And for versatility, the writer added, Jackie beat them all. His name was also mentioned in connection with Red Grange and with perhaps the greatest American athlete, Native American Jim Thorpe.

It was quite a comedown to go from such triumphs to the anonymity of being a counselor in a camp in the boondocks. Everything that was absurd and self-destructive about segregation was revealed here. Because of an obsession with skin color and race, a powerful modern nation was depriving itself of the services of an exciting and talented individual.

4

ARMY BLUES
(1941-1944)

Working at the NYA camp was Jackie's first adult job. The job was fine but the pay was not. He made some extra money playing with a barnstorming football team, the Los Angeles Bulldogs. This small amount of playing made him want to make regular use of his athletic skills. There were no blacks in the National Football League (NFL), but the semipro Honolulu Bears was an integrated team. So Jackie sailed to Hawaii to get a football job.

He played with the team on weekends. To make extra money, weekdays were spent working for a construction company on a site near Pearl Harbor. Though he was a popular player, both were dead-end jobs. He decided it would be better to return to the NYA, a decision that came none too soon. Had he remained a little longer, he might have been killed in the Japanese surprise attack on Pearl Harbor that thrust America into World War II. As it was, he sailed out of Hawaii on December 5, 1941, only two days before the Pearl Harbor bombing.

War brought a dilemma. Large numbers of young men were volunteering or being drafted for service in the armed forces. Jackie had a legitimate reason for being exempted from the draft: He still had bone chips as a result of the ankle broken in college. On the other hand, people would ask how an all-around athlete was not in good enough physical condition to serve his country in its hour of need. A compromise was worked out. Jackie was drafted in early 1942 for "limited service." He was sent to Fort Riley, Kansas, where he had to learn, of all things, to handle horses in a cavalry unit.

In those days, the U.S. Army was segregated. For the first time in his life, Jackie ran into official second-class citizenship as part of daily routine. With his college education, he felt he could do better than be a low-ranked soldier. So when he finished basic training, he tried to enter Officers Candidate School, only to be told that there was no room for any more blacks.

Other blacks accepted such an answer as a fact of life and shrugged it off. Not Jackie. He had his pride. It just so happened that the most famous black man in the world, boxing heavyweight champion Joe Louis, was at Fort Riley just then. On hearing of Jackie's trouble, Louis pulled a few wires, and Jackie got into the officers' school.

Commissioned as a second lieutenant in January 1943, he was made morale officer at Fort Riley. Once again he ran into prejudice, and once again he rocked the boat. Because he was black, he was not allowed to play on the Fort Riley baseball team, but the football team was integrated and the officers were eager for Jackie to play football. He refused to play football if he could not play baseball. The white officers would not give in, and he was told that he had not made himself popular by his "antics."

Nor was that the only incident. Black soldiers were being victimized by separate and unequal facilities in the Army Post Exchange (PX), the military store and snack shop. Because of too few seats in the "colored" section, they often had to stand, even though many seats were empty in the "white" section. Black officers accepted this setup—until Jackie came along. He started to make phone calls, trying to change things. A major said to him over the phone, "How would you like to have your wife sitting next to a nigger?"

Jack blew up. He reported the remark to a sympathetic colonel. As a result, blacks received more chairs in their section of the PX. The place remained segregated, but at least something had been changed by taking a stand. The price paid was that such assertive actions marked him again as a "troublemaker," an "uppity nigger." His justification was that, as morale officer, he was supposed to attend to the problems that affected the black soldiers' morale. The seating in the PX certainly did that.

Jackie's next assignment was to an all-black tank battalion in Camp Hood, Texas, deep in the segregated South. There he frankly told the sergeant and the soldiers that he knew nothing about tanks. As the officer in charge he would depend on them for guidance and hard work. This forthrightness worked. The men obtained the best rating of any unit for readiness and efficiency.

The colonel in charge was eager to send Jackie abroad with his battalion in spite of the ankle injury. But then the explosive combination of southern racism, army legalism, and Jackie's combativeness ignited again. Jackie was on a bus talking to a very light-skinned black woman of his acquaintance. According to Texas laws, blacks were supposed to sit in the back of the bus. According to army regulations, seating was not segregated. The driver, a local civilian, thought that the woman Jackie was talking to was white. Such casualness violated local custom. The outraged driver ordered Jackie to the back of the bus.

Jackie knew his rights on an army base. It was only recently that Joe Louis and another black boxer, Sugar Ray Robinson, had refused to move to the back of buses, and that bad publicity had forced the army to forbid racial discrimination in vehicles on army posts. Jackie would not move. The driver boiled.

On reaching the last stop, the bus driver quickly brought over several white men and two military policemen. The MPs took Jackie to a captain, who saw in him only an "uppity nigger" trying to make trouble. He filed a series of charges against Jackie. That meant he would be court-martialed, that is, tried before a court of officers. One of the charges was drunkenness, though Jackie had never had an alcoholic drink in his life.

Jackie did not take this incident passively. He made sure that other black officers heard of it. They in turn contacted black newspapers and civil rights groups, who demanded an airing of the facts. This publicity forced the army to drop the worst charges, but it insisted that Jackie go on trial for the lesser charges.

The trial took place in August 1944. Jackie's defense attorney had little trouble showing that the testimony of the captain and the two military policemen was full of holes and contradictions. The verdict came down, not guilty. Jackie felt relieved at being vindicated but disgusted wth the army's stupidity in letting the case come to trial in the first place. The army officials were not happy at having pie on their faces. Jackie and the U.S. Army were growing less and less fond of each other.

The one thing that relieved the boredom and irritations of army service in the remoter parts of Kansas and Texas was writing letters to Rachel. They had known each other for four years but lately had seen little of each other, although they had become engaged in early 1943, at the time Jackie became a second lieutenant. They planned to marry when she finished school, but he was far away, and she had moved to San Francisco to complete her nursing education. Her roommates and friends were dating a lot of servicemen and having wartime romances. She was not sure whether she had done the right thing in choosing Jackie when she was so young and there was fun to be had in wartime San Francisco.

Then she wrote him that she was thinking of going

into the Women's Cadet Corps. An angry Jackie, with strong ideas about a woman's proper place, wrote back that maybe their engagement was a mistake. Too proud to be bossed around, Rachel promptly returned his bracelet and engagement ring. Both Jackie and Rachel were miserable. Jackie even gave the bracelet to a girl from a nearby Texas town, whom he dated for a while. Yet he kept on writing to Rachel. And she, though hurt that he would give the bracelet to another woman, kept on answering.

Jackie, home on leave, was depressed. But at his mother's suggestion, he called Rachel. He could tell from the sound of her voice that she was happy to hear him. He rushed to San Francisco, and they had a joyous reunion.

Life in the army had proved to be dull and irritating. Instead of fighting the Japanese or German enemy, Jackie had to fight the racism and stupidity of his fellow Americans. Even though he was acquitted in the court-martial, he now requested to be released from military service because of his ankle. He cut through the chain of command and wrote special delivery to the adjutant general in Washington asking for a discharge. Jackie hoped that his court-martial would encourage the army to get rid of someone it saw as a problem.

The army transferred him to a Kentucky post. He went home on furlough and then visited Rachel in San Francisco. They were happy to be reunited, but not ready to be engaged again. Still, Jackie returned to Kentucky full of hope. In November 1944, after he was at the new army post only a short while, he received his honorable discharge from the army for medical reasons.

While he was waiting to be released, Jackie happened to be walking past a recreational field on the post. A baseball bounced near him. As many passersby might do, he caught it and threw it to the baseball player chasing it. It was a neat one-handed catch and a perfect throw. The player did a double take. He asked if Jackie had ever played ball. Jackie told him of his UCLA days. The player had heard of Jackie as a football and track star, not a baseball one.

The player turned out to have been a pitcher for the Kansas City Monarchs in the Negro Baseball League. He urged Jackie to apply to that team.

Jackie was in fact facing the problem of finding something to do once he was discharged. Even after three years in the army all he had was a roomful of trophies, no career. He wrote to the Monarchs organization and received an invitation to try out the next spring. In the meantime, the minister of Jackie's church in Pasadena had become president of Sam Houston State College, a small black school in Texas. He offered Jackie a job as basketball coach. The offer and the timing were perfect. Jackie had been looking forward to some sort of coaching career, and he had no other source of income till spring training with the Monarchs began. He took the coaching job as soon as he was released from the army.

The three years of boredom and tensions in the army were ended. Prospects suddenly opened all around him: a fall and winter coaching job available right away; good chances of a professional baseball job in the spring and summer; a wonderful girlfriend still waiting for him in California; and, now that he had jobs, the likelihood of marriage at last.

Once out of the army, Jackie rushed back to Los Angeles, where Rachel was now working. There they spent some of the happiest days of their lives. They became engaged again and planned their wedding. Almost overnight Jackie's life had turned around.

5

BLACKBALL

(1945)

At Sam Houston State College, Jackie did a fine job coaching the team. It even managed to beat the previous year's league champion in one of its games. The pay, though, was terribly low, and he resigned the job. He did well in the tryouts held by the Monarchs in April 1945. The organization offered him $400 a month. To a black man seeking to start a career, that was decent money then. It was not major league baseball, though; it was the Negro League.

In its professional form baseball has been around for more than a century, since 1869. In those first years, there was an occasional black player, but organized baseball developed in the very period in which second-class citizenship for the newly freed black slaves was being established all over the South. Blacks became excluded from baseball as from much else then, and by 1887 the game was all white.

After a scandal involving gambling and fixed games with the Chicago White Sox in 1919, the baseball owners established the post of commissioner. The first to hold that post, Judge K. M. Landis, was a tough Southerner who held the office for twenty-five years and saw to it that blacks could not enter baseball. As a result, black baseball players formed all-black teams that earned money by "barnstorming," that is, they traveled from town to town and staged games with local players. Gradually the Negro Baseball League was formed with something resembling schedules, club standings, and statistics.

One of the excuses for keeping blacks out of major league play was that they were inferior as athletes and as team players and that they "choked" under the pressure of competitive play. Yet, curiously, in exhibition games between black and white all-star teams, the black teams won more often than the white ones. Black players and reporters naturally drew the conclusion that the best black players were at least as good as the best major leaguers. But how, with a segregated America, could they ever prove their point?

Though black talent was obviously out there, not many owners—or players, fans, or reporters—were eager to change things. The owners, besides sharing in the general prejudice, were afraid that integration would cost them business by driving away white fans without bringing in enough black ones to make up the difference.

A few prominent white sportswriters and a lot of black ones decried the absence of blacks from baseball. They were responding to the breakthrough made by blacks in other sports—in boxing (Joe Louis), track

(Jesse Owens), and college football (many players). Nothing much might have changed had it not been for the coming of World War II.

Fighting Nazi racism in Europe made Americans, black and white, conscious of racism at home. How could America stand for freedom abroad while it had second-class citizenship at home? Race riots in 1943 in New York, Detroit, and in Texas resulted in early, mild desegregation moves by President Roosevelt. In 1944, segregation of baseball fans by race in the major league baseball parks was discontinued.

When Commissioner Landis died that same year, black journalists and activists felt that the time had come to make a big push for integrating baseball. The selection of another Southerner as new commissioner, Senator A. B. Chandler of Kentucky, at first seemed a setback to their cause. To their surprise, however, he came out in favor of integration.

In 1945, both in New York and in Boston, politicians running for office were trying to win black votes by insisting on integrated hometown teams. With so much pressure on them, the Boston Red Sox decided to hold a mock tryout for blacks in April 1945. Jackie had barely started training with the Monarchs when he received a call from a black editor asking him to go to Boston with two other players. They arrived, did their thing, left, and did not get any offers. Someone had yelled, "Get those niggers off the field!"

Around the same time, another sportswriter went with a different group of black players to the Brooklyn Dodger training camp in Bear Mountain, New York, and demanded a tryout for them. Branch Rickey, the general manager, was angry. They were ruining his carefully laid plans to bring a black into the majors. As he sent them away, he said that he was committed to their cause, but using pressure tactics was self-defeating. The black journalist had heard such paternalistic expressions of sympathy too many times before to believe it.

Little did they know that Rickey was telling the truth and that he had already started the process of bringing a black into baseball. He prepared for such a major breakthrough with all the care and secrecy that was being put into the development of the first atomic bomb.

Blacks forcing white teams to hire them, he believed, was not the right way. No matter how good their cause or claim, they would only earn hatred. Integration had to be brought about by white society itself. Rickey had a master plan.

Wesley Branch Rickey, from Ohio, was articulate, devoutly religious, and college educated. After a brief fling at major league baseball and at being a country lawyer, he found that his real talent lay in running a baseball team. He was a genius at it, perhaps the greatest in the history of the game. He was a brilliant judge of talent and an innovator without peer. After building a powerful team in St. Louis, he went to Brooklyn in 1942. There his daring moves prepared the ground for the great Dodger teams of 1947–1956.

One of those innovations was to bring a black man into baseball. The black athlete's talent would assure a Dodger championship, and his presence would raise attendance figures by bringing more black spectators to the ballpark. Rickey's desire to win and his love of money combined with his decency to make him try to open the doors of baseball to the excluded.

As early as 1943 he secretly revealed to some important people his radical idea. He read up on history and sociology. He consulted experts in race relations theory. Then at a press conference in May 1945, he announced that he felt the Negro League was poorly run. He was therefore going to establish a new black "United States League" and would begin a great talent search for it.

Many black sportswriters, who had attended the conference expecting an important announcement, were deeply disappointed. It looked like another white man's trick to keep blacks out of major league baseball. They were half right. It was a trick, all right, but one meant to get blacks *into* organized baseball.

The reactions of the few people to whom Rickey revealed his secret were ominous. His family thought it was a good idea best left to someone else to undertake. The baseball owners and executives did not even think it a good idea. Red Barber, the great and popular radio broadcaster of Dodger games, was stunned. His first impulse was to resign his job.

From these reactions Rickey could tell that if word leaked out, steps might be taken in baseball to prevent the Dodgers from carrying out his plans. Secrecy was also necessary if the best possible player was to be tracked down. By talking about forming a new Negro league, Rickey put everyone off-guard. The big league scouts, many of them Southerners, might have sabotaged the plan if they knew of it. Instead they studied black players in the United States, Mexico, Cuba, and Puerto Rico for what they thought would be a "Brown Dodgers" team.

Rickey wanted a pool of the best black players to be made available to the Dodgers. From that pool he would pick the one who would be a trailblazer. He had, of course, to be an excellent ballplayer, but that was only the beginning. He had to have a model lifestyle off the playing field. He had to be an intelligent, presentable person who would look comfortable in a three-piece suit and while speaking to the press. He had also to be a man with a sense of mission, a crusader willing to rock the boat. He had to have reserves of patience and endurance. He had to be able to handle the adulation of blacks and the hatred of whites without striking back or striking out.

Above all, he had to perform a delicate balancing act; he had to go in two directions at once. On the one hand, he had to feel enough outrage at injustice to be willing to do something about it. On the other hand, he had to refrain from temper tantrums and violence. He had to assert his rights and his dignity in a civilized way.

The first black man in baseball would be taunted

and yelled at everywhere. He would be called every name in the book. How many athletes, no matter how gentlemanly in behavior, could stay cool and resist the temptation to lash out? Even if he did remain in control, his teammates, his opponents, and the people in the stands might not. All these others would see his forbearance as cowardice and would urge him to strike back.

Rickey had every aspect of the outstanding black players looked into. This one was too old, that one too young and immature. For a while, the search narrowed down to Roy Campanella and Jackie Robinson. Then important differences became clear. Campanella had dropped out of school to join the Negro League at the age of fifteen; Jackie had gone to college. Furthermore, Jackie had always played on integrated teams. Many of the Negro League players, like Campanella, were used to taking orders from white people, not playing alongside them. They lacked the experience and self-possession needed at this juncture.

The finger of fate was pointing at Jackie Robinson, shortstop for the Kansas City Monarchs. Rickey asked a black sportswriter whether any of the three who participated in the Boston tryout were good. The reporter answered, "Jack Robinson." Scouting reports were unanimous about Jackie's skills. The only problem was his throwing arm—not strong enough for shortstop but good enough for second base.

There was still the matter of Jackie's character. Rickey himself went to California to find out firsthand about Jackie from the people who knew him at school. What he heard satisfied him. He did not smoke, drink, or womanize. He could express himself clearly and wittily. He had played with whites. He had been an army officer. He had leadership qualities and the courage to fight for his beliefs. He had independence and resilience. Unwilling to accept the racism he had run into all his life, he had a strong need to be accepted at his true worth as a first-class citizen. He was someone who would work for his cause—that of blacks and of America—as well as for himself and his team. In short, though not necessarily the best black baseball player, he was the best choice for this great innovation.

On the other hand, Jackie had left behind him a trail of observations about him as arrogant and troublemaking, a "racial agitator" who talked back and insisted on his constitutional rights. There had been the arrest at UCLA, the court-martial in the army. He was not one to get along by going along. He was not a Southern black taught to know his place. He had a Californian's big expectations from life.

Rickey was sensitive. He knew more about black people, Jackie later said, than any other white man; he was the "Einstein of baseball integration." Where others saw signs of an "uppity nigger," Rickey saw that these actions, if performed by a white man, would have earned him praise as dynamic, gutsy, individualistic.

Here, then, was the man with the qualities to undertake a crusade. In his school days, Jackie established himself as an athlete. In his army days, he established himself as a fighter for civil rights. Now he would get a chance to combine the two phases of his life, the two themes of his career. Rickey seemed to have found his man at last.

But there would be one final test.

6

FROM MONARCH TO ROYAL
(1945-1946)

Branch Rickey caught up with Jackie at an unhappy stage of his life. The high hopes he had at the time of his release from the army had fizzled in a few months. The coaching job had not worked out financially, and that was supposed to be his career. Black baseball was a miserable way to make a living. The pay was low. The travel schedule was hectic, filled with long bus trips and doubleheaders. Decent hotels for blacks were hard to find. Rarely could one sit down in a good restaurant for a leisurely hot meal. He found it hard to accept the humiliating segregation in the southern towns in the casual way other team members did.

Worst of all, Rachel had expected him, once out of the army, to settle in California. Instead, he found himself in a dilemma: either make a living by being far away for a long time or be near his girlfriend and his mother but without a good job prospect. He wrote frequent letters to Rachel from depressing, distant places, but after six years their future together looked hopeless.

It was when Jackie was in this rut, playing with the Monarchs in Chicago in August 1945, that one of Rickey's scouts contacted him and brought him back to New York. The scout himself was wondering why so much concern was being shown over whether a black shortstop had a throwing arm good enough for a new Brown Dodgers team.

On August 28, 1945, Jackie and the scout entered Rickey's office in Brooklyn. A new era in sports was about to begin. During the next three hours took place one of the great scenes in American and in sports history.

As was his habit, Rickey stared at the man in order to size him up. Jackie was handsome, broad shouldered, almost six feet tall. His skin was extremely dark. (That ruled out any question of a light-skinned black man passing for, or being acceptable as, a white man.) He weighed 195 pounds. He had a pigeon-toed walk. His face showed intelligence and sensitivity. He spoke carefully and sounded educated. One could not tell over the phone that he was black, yet when angry he could hurl ghetto epithets with the best of them. His eyes and gestures radiated a certain intensity and determination that were the hallmarks of his style.

After some small talk, Rickey's first question was, "Do you have a girlfriend?" That seemed an unusual question for a stranger to ask. Besides, Jackie was not even sure whether he did or did not. He told the story of his roller coaster love life with Rachel. Rickey commented: "You know you have a girl. When we get through today you may want to call her up because there are times when a man needs a woman by his side."

Now Jackie became more suspicious and curious and excited. Soon enough, Rickey revealed his great secret: Jackie was being considered not for any Negro League team but for the Brooklyn Dodgers. Jackie was stunned.

Rickey had thoroughly investigated Jackie. His conclusion was that he was enough of a ballplayer for the job. The only question that remained was: Did Jackie have the guts for it? "There's virtually nobody on our side. No owners or umpires, few newspapermen or fans. We can win only if you're a great ballplayer and fine gentleman." The first part, about being a ballplayer, would be easy. That is only a matter, Rickey explained, of "hits, runs, and errors, because the baseball box score is a democratic thing." It does not show skin color. Baseball is more than a box score, though. It is presence on the field. There skin color mattered. Did Jackie have guts?

Jackie was challenged. Of course he had guts! He did not think he could take harassment passively—or should. "Mr. Rickey, are you looking for a Negro who is afraid to fight back?"

Rickey waved his cigar and answered in mock anger: "I'm looking for a player with guts enough *not* to fight back!"

After a pause, Jackie said: "Oh, I get it, Mr. Rickey. You want me to turn the other cheek."

Jackie was being asked to put his pride as a man and as a black on hold, not just for himself but for all potential black players. Fighting was not the answer, not with so many people on the other side. If someone cursed or hit Jackie, he might think it right to hit back, but it would defeat the experiment. Jackie would have to turn the other cheek even though that went against his nature. That would not be cowardice; that would be heroism.

A lot was at stake. Rickey reminded Jackie that wherever he went, he would collect abuse from opposing players, fans, waiters, clerks, maybe even some teammates. On the playing field, racial slurs would be the least of it. There would be beanballs from pitchers. Players would slide into bases with spikes high or with the aim of knocking him over. Fans would throw things at him from the stands.

Rickey acted out these scenes. He called Jackie every insulting name and pictured for him the rough play on the field: the deliberate collision, the cry of "dirty nigger!" He waved his fist in Jackie's face, an inch from his nose. Again and again the question was, Could Jackie take it? Could he grin and bear it without fighting back?

It was hard enough for Jackie to restrain himself here and now as Rickey conjured up the scenes.

"Can you do it? I know you are naturally combative. But for three years you will have to do it the only way it can be done. Can you do it?"

A minute passed as Jackie looked at Rickey in silence. Finally he said tensely, "Mr. Rickey, I've got to do it. If you want to take this gamble, I promise you there'll be no incidents."

Rickey sat back and breathed a sigh of relief. Jackie had passed the last test. Jackie understood. The alliance was formed. The experiment was under way. Rickey and Jackie became friends for the rest of their lives.

All that was left was to clear up the terms of the arrangement. Jackie would need at least one year of seasoning, as do nearly all players, at an International League (Class AAA) farm club before entering the major leagues. The Dodgers' farm club was in Montreal. Jackie would make $600 a month playing for the Montreal Royals, plus a bonus of $3,500 for signing. He was to reveal all this only to his mother and his girlfriend.

On October 23, 1945, Jackie met in Montreal with the officials of the Dodgers and the Royals to sign a contract with Montreal. At a press conference, the world first heard that a black man was going to play in organized baseball. Jackie was introduced to the reporters. He came across as friendly and articulate.

He had a lot of searching questions to answer. He said that he was proud to be "doing something" for his race in breaking the color line. He would try to carry on the great job Joe Louis had been doing. He foresaw no difficulties, as most of his athletic experience had been with racially mixed teams. As far as off-the-field problems were concerned, he was ready to take his chances.

The announcement sent shock waves through the

sports world and society at large. Even people not interested in baseball took one side or the other. Many baseball people were angered. They predicted that no good could come of this experiment. Minor league officials, who would be the first to confront the problem of a black in their midst, were especially unhappy. The *Sporting News*, a leading publication, was certain that the wrong thing was being done. The white owners of the Kansas City Monarchs, backed by the major league owners, tried in vain to keep Jackie by claiming that he was under contract with them.

The new baseball commissioner, Happy Chandler, remained silent. A committee of major league officials wrote a report that saw no need for blacks in baseball. They feared legal problems. They feared that black athletes were unprepared for the majors. They feared financial losses for all concerned. Some people hid their racism by claiming that the problem was not with signing up a black man but with signing up *this* black man, who came trailing clouds of troublemaking. Others worried that Jackie had achieved stardom in football and basketball. As a baseball player, they said, he was not good enough for the majors. This was the belief of pitching great Bob Feller, who said that Jackie had the torso of a football player, not a batter.

More unsettling was the fact that the blacks who played with Jackie did not think of him as the best player in the Negro League. As a result, some blacks thought that this was really yet another in a long series of tricks and delaying actions by the white baseball establishment. They thought that Jackie had been signed on purpose in order to have him fail and to set back the cause of integrating baseball.

Not all reaction was negative, even in the South. Some newspapers went so far as to compare Rickey to Lincoln. Lincoln had freed the black man, and now Rickey was freeing the black athlete.

That winter was filled with rumors about moves by officials or players to prevent integration. It was also filled with signs that hiring Jackie was causing America to examine its conscience and its rules concerning the treatment of races on the playing field. Other professional sports, especially football and basketball, were starting to lower the color barrier. Even without playing one inning, Jackie and Rickey had already begun a quiet revolution. Though baseball is only a game, it is also more than a game. In the lives of Americans, it is something almost as serious as politics or religion.

For Jackie, the signing was not just an opportunity to change the face of America. It was also an opportunity to change the drift of his private life. Here at long last was a job that would enable him to marry the woman he had loved for six years. Rachel had herself recently gotten a job in New York, even as Jackie was being hired by a New York organization. Their lives were converging in more ways than one.

Jackie had committed himself to a barnstorming tour of Venezuela on an all-star Negro team, so from November 1945 to January 1946 he was in South America. Even there he was sought after for interviews. A comic book with the story of his life appeared. He had become famous overnight.

Rachel had promised to marry him as soon as he returned from that trip. When the barnstorming tour was over, the couple returned to California. They were married there on February 10, 1946. After a honeymoon of a few weeks in San Jose and Oakland, they got ready for spring training.

Rachel had never been in the South and had little idea of what life was like for blacks living under segregation. The trip to Florida for spring training was quite an introduction for her. They had to take a number of different flights, and, because they were black, they were bumped for white passengers. They had to wait long hours in the confined black sections of the airports, often with no decent food or hotel room available. They had to endure a sixteen-hour ride in uncomfortable seats in the rear of a bus while the comfortable reclining seats in the white section remained empty. She had to worry over Jackie controlling his temper whenever he ran into racial insults, especially to his new wife.

7

SPRINGTIME DEBUT
(1946)

Spring training was going to be an ordeal. Even in a normal year, there were hundreds of players competing for the chance to make it into the majors or into a Class AAA minor league team. This year it was far more difficult. With World War II ending the summer before, many major league players had returned from military service eager to regain their positions on the Dodgers and the Royals. At the age of 27, Jackie had to compete with men his age who were experienced in major league play and with inexperienced but talented, eager players who were a decade younger than he. And then, of course, there was the racial matter.

Before Jackie arrived, Rickey addressed the assembled Dodgers and would-be Dodgers. He told them that his only goal was to get a winning team. A man's performance on the field was all that mattered. In order to lighten the tremendous burden on Jackie, Rickey had also signed a black pitcher, Johnny

Wright, and he hired two black journalists to accompany them through spring training. Jackie would have at least one companion on the field. But Wright was only an afterthought. The spotlight was on the breakthrough man, Jackie Robinson.

The first day Jackie showed up at the training camp was scary. Here were all those men practicing on the field, many from the South, all of them white. Suddenly everyone seemed to stop and stare at the two black men who had just arrived. There were press photographers insisting that Jackie pose in all sorts of ways. Reporters from all over the nation bombarded Jackie with questions, which he managed to answer with intelligence and humor. He was asked, for instance, what he would do if a pitcher threw a beanball at him. "I would duck," he replied matter-of-factly, and everyone laughed.

Another ordeal was meeting the newly hired manager of the Royals, Clay Hopper. The man was a plantation owner from Mississippi. Rickey hoped to show that if a Mississippian could learn to live with Jackie on the team, anyone could. A prosperous man who did not need this job, Hopper already knew of the Robinson signing when he agreed to manage the team. He was loyal to Rickey and his plans. When he saw Jackie for the first time, he said, "Well, when Mr. Rickey picked one, he sure picked a black one."

The ice was broken when Hopper greeted Jackie with a cheerful "hello" and shook his hand. Many Southerners would not have done even that. Throughout the spring, Hopper played his role well. He treated the two blacks on the team fairly. At the end of spring training, he called Jackie "a regular fella and a regular member of my baseball club." He was notably proud of Jackie's fielding and baserunning.

Jackie was so eager to make good that in practice sessions he threw the ball as hard as he could. Sure enough, in a few hours his arm was sore. Rickey wanted Jackie to be getting the same testing as any other player. To have Jackie now be out because of a sore arm would make it look as though he got the job just because of his skin color.

Rickey needed Jackie to be playing somewhere. He had planned, because Jackie's weakness as a player was his arm, to make Jackie a second baseman rather than a shortstop. But now, with the arm sore, even second base was a problem, and Rickey tried to make Jackie a first baseman overnight. Not used to the position, Jackie played awkwardly there at first. Some hostile newspapermen and players indeed felt that if he had been white, he'd never have been picked.

Rickey expected much from Jackie's baserunning abilities and actively participated in the practice sessions. "Be more daring," he yelled at Jackie on base. He urged him to take a bigger lead, to take chances and run, to annoy the pitcher.

Before the first exhibition game, Jackie was a bundle of nerves. When he stepped out on the field for the first time, he expected a salvo of insults from the mostly white Florida spectators. Instead he heard only a few scattered boos. A sharp play at his position brought him a burst of applause. From then on, he was less nervous.

Nevertheless, things did not go easily. Many towns in the South did not want racially mixed teams. Exhibition games were canceled in Jacksonville and De Land, Florida; Savannah, Georgia; and Richmond, Virginia. In a game at Sanford, Florida, no sooner had Jackie scored in a close play at home in the first inning than he was ordered removed by the local police.

The Dodger officials took a hard line. Either Jackie was allowed to play or there would be no game. To let the game go on without the team's black man would be to encourage racists everywhere.

In the town where the Dodgers had their training camp, Daytona Beach, the local officials were cooperative and the fans delighted. Jackie was able to play in exhibition games on the home grounds without any problem. The Daytona Beach folks were smart enough to see that hosting the Dodger organization at a time when the eyes of the nation, and especially of its largest city, were on Jackie was a lot of free publicity for their town as a winter resort area. The Dodgers presence also brought extra business to the town. This helped teach some Southern officials and businessmen to overlook, at least sometimes, the color of a person's skin. That lesson gradually spread to the rest of baseball and, years later, became a theme of the civil rights movement. After establishing that blacks had the same abilities as whites, integration would be seen to also make economic sense.

In early games, when Jackie came to the plate or onto the field, he received cheers rather than boos. Much of that came of course from the black section of the stands. As his talents blossomed, quite a surprising amount came from the white section too. White fans started to pour in for the exhibition games as if to see a freak show. More and more they cheered Jackie, giving the lie to the officials who had repeatedly said that they would love to integrate the game but the fans would not put up with it.

Rickey's strategy was working. A few courageous blacks, cooperating with and tutored by a few sympathetic whites, confronted segregation. By refusing to leave the blacks behind, the whites forced the local officials, concerned with the money baseball brought in, to back off.

Another widespread fear proved groundless: Jackie ran into little hostility among the players, even those whose position he was in competition for. His teammates played it cool. They did not support him; they did not oppose him. They just allowed the testing of his abilities to take its own course. Some Southerners were aloof at first but quickly came around. Jackie's charm helped win some over; his skills won over others. One Southern pitcher threw beanballs twice when Jackie was at bat, and each time Jackie got up and proceeded to get a hit. The pitcher later said to manager Hopper, "Clay, your colored boy is going to do all right."

After the experiment with first base, Jackie was switched back to second. More at ease here, he made some great plays. Yet, though his fielding and baserunning were excellent, his hitting was not. In squad games he went hitless for long stretches. The consensus was that he was a poor hitter because he lunged at the ball. He had to make do on bunts and infield hits if he was to get a chance to show his baserunning abilities.

By the end of spring training, his arm had healed, and he was beginning to hit. Though he had not had a chance to play much at second base, he showed a great capacity to learn and an eagerness to do so. He had earned his position in the lineup and in the field. Rickey had reasons to feel good about having signed him and about ignoring all the baleful predictions.

Jackie's career had begun with a baptism of fire in the Deep South. At long last came the middle of April and the end of *that* ordeal. Opening day for the Montreal Royals was in Jersey City on April 14, 1946. It was the beginning of the first season since the war ended. In the holiday-like atmosphere, schoolchildren were given the day off. More journalists were present than at any major league team's opening day. Jackie heard from the manager that he would bat second and play second base. This time it was for real. He was going to play in organized baseball, the first black to do so in this century. "Another Emancipation Day" someone called it.

After the leadoff batter grounded out, Jackie came to the plate. The crowd greeted him politely. He had butterflies in his stomach. His knees were weak, his hands so wet that he could hardly hold on to the bat. It is not easy to step into the batter's box knowing you are making history and carrying a whole race of people on your back. It is bad enough just being a rookie.

He took the first five pitches. He swung at the sixth. It was a ground ball to shortstop. He was easily thrown out. As he came back to the dugout, the crowd cheered as if he had hit a home run. He sat down, as relieved as they were that that symbolic first step was behind him.

Judging by his second at bat, he must have been very relieved. It was the third inning, and the Royals had gotten two men on base. The situation called for Jackie, a skilled bunter, to do so. The infield moved in. The pitcher threw high, hoping to make him pop up in the bunt attempt. Jackie outwitted him, however, and swung away. The sound and the feel of the contact of bat with ball, plus the roar of the crowd, told him he had connected. A three-run homer! When he returned to the dugout, even Southern teammates patted him on the back. "That's the way to hit 'em, Jackie!"

On his next at bat, he went the other way, by bunting just when they expected him to swing away again. With his great speed, he easily beat out the throw. Now came his first opportunity as a base runner. Rickey had thoroughly trained him to drive the pitchers crazy with daring on the bases. Jackie took a long lead and then dived back as the catcher faked a throw to first. Before the next pitch, Jackie again jumped way off first base, but this time he kept going and stole second with ease.

Now he played the same daring game at second. The next batter hit a ground ball to third base. In such a case, the correct thing is for the runner to stay at second. Jackie pretended to return to second but then did the unorthodox thing: When the third baseman threw to first, Jackie took off for third. He just barely beat the throw from first to third.

Now he started dancing off third base. Several times the pitcher threw to third, forcing Jackie back. Then, when the pitcher finally pitched, Jackie bluffed running home but returned to third. When he started toward home again and suddenly stopped, the pitcher was so distracted that he stopped in the middle of the next pitch. The umpire called a balk, and Jackie walked home. He had not stolen home; he had only extorted it from the pitcher.

The crowd was delirious. They had just seen daring baseball at its best. Running hard had gotten him to first base, by beating out the bunt. Running hard had gotten him to second on a steal. Running hard and shrewdly had gotten him to third by outwitting the fielders. And running hard and shrewdly had gotten him home by outwitting, confusing, distracting, and enraging the pitcher. He had circled the bases on skill and nerves and speed, unlike his previous home run, with its relatively dull free ride. It was a tremendous display of the two opposite ways of scoring. The home run was more productive, but the running game was much more exciting. In any case, the crowd loved both.

Montreal won the game easily, 14–1. Jackie had four hits in five at bats, one of those hits the three-run homer. He stole two bases and batted in three runs. He scored four runs, two of them on pitchers' balks caused by his dashes from third. It was a spectacular opening day performance for anyone, rookie or veteran, first black or familiar white. That Jackie also happened to be the first black in organized baseball made it all seem unbelievably corny and movielike. Actually, those who had followed Jackie's career were not surprised. He always was at his best when something important was on the line.

A black journalist wrote of the black man proving himself worthy in the "crucible of white-hot competition" and of "the most significant sports story of the century." A little more low key was the reaction of the proud originator of this experiment, Branch Rickey. He did not attend the game because he did not want to add to the pressure Jackie was feeling. He was instead at a midtown New York restaurant giving a small dinner party for a group that included broadcaster Red Barber. As the group was entering the restaurant, an assistant of Rickey's rushed over to him, in a state of excitement.

"Mr. Rickey! . . . Jackie Robinson"— he stopped to catch his breath—"Mr. Rickey, Jackie came up in the third inning with two men on and hit a home run!"

"He did?"

"Yes . . . and, Mr. Rickey, he got three singles and stole two bases."

As the group continued into the restaurant, Rickey touched Barber's elbow and said, "Now, that's a pretty good way to break into organized baseball."

8

MONTREAL
(1946)

The three-game series in Jersey City brought out large crowds. Integration had been a success at the box office, against all predictions, just as it had been on the playing field. There was no brawling and no racial tension. The success went beyond the box office. After each game, the fans tried to touch Jackie, as if he were a movie idol or music superstar.

That was fun, but the ghosts of spring training returned to haunt him now. The next stop on the road trip was Baltimore, a city with a Deep South atmosphere. Officials there warned Rickey of either violence or a boycott. Large crowds, blacks and whites, showed up. No boycott, then, but what of the other possibility? Rachel, sitting near the Montreal dugout, heard someone shout, "Here comes that nigger son of a bitch. Let's give it to him now!" She was in tears. She wondered if the experiment was a mistake.

Despite the fears and the racist slurs, nothing happened. In the first two games, Jackie did not hit well, and he committed two errors, one of them costing the game. If the fears and the pressure had gotten through to him, he managed to overcome them in the third game. He had three hits in three at bats and scored four runs.

During the two weeks of the road trip, Jackie got at least one hit in ten of the twelve games, for a .372 average. On the bases, he was phenomenal: He stole eight bases and scored seventeen runs. And now at last the team was off to its hometown, Montreal.

The Dodgers were well suited to break the color line. The flagship of the Dodger farm system was the Montreal team. The city of Montreal was perfect for inaugurating the integration of baseball because it was part of less color-conscious Canada. It is, of course, ironic and shameful that the integration of America's pastime had to be started in another country.

Jackie and Rachel now needed to find a place to live. They finally settled on an apartment in a French-speaking neighborhood. Not too many blacks lived in Canada, and none in that area. The Robinsons were therefore the objects of curiosity. Aware that history was being made by the black man in their midst, the neighbors followed Jackie's every movement. As Rachel was pregnant, they were eager to be helpful.

The season got into full gear, and Jackie found that wherever he went the cheers and adulation were mixed with curses and jeers from players and fans. Inevitably, there were beanballs from pitchers. He stood his ground and ducked. Instead of losing his temper, the better reaction was to get a hit. At second base he was often the target of the spikes of sliding runners.

What enabled Jackie to handle the rough play at second was partly his football experience, which had made him used to body contact, and partly his competitive spirit. Sliding spikes first into second was regular high-intensity baseball. He himself did it when he stole bases, and he was prepared to have others do it to him when he was in the field. Race need not have anything to do with it. That was the competitive attitude he used as psychological armor.

As Jackie held up under both the stress of dodging beanballs and the injuries from spikes, his teammates came to have greater respect for him. The Royals players, even the Southerners, began to see him as a productive player rather than as a black man. The thawing of relations was helped by his charm and by his key role in many victories. Rickey's prediction was coming true: On the playing field, skin color was less important than winning. Gradually, he started to join the players at the meal table and to play cards with them. Hopper, the manager from Mississippi, was impressed and saw in him "a great ballplayer."

While Jackie was at Montreal, Roy Campanella and Don Newcombe, who were signed up with a lot less fuss soon after Jackie, were playing at a Class B minor league team, in Nashua, New Hampshire. Like secret agents in an alien land, the three men kept in contact throughout the baseball season to exchange ideas and compare experiences. Jackie's challenges at Montreal were uppermost in their minds, for he was at the cutting edge of progress.

If Montreal, a foreign city, felt like home, some American cities felt like enemy country. Syracuse, New York, though a northern city, proved to have players as unfriendly as any southern ones. And there was always Baltimore.

During the second trip to that city, on the last play of a game, a fight broke out on the field (not involving Jackie), and fans rushed to the support of their Orioles. They pushed their way to the dressing room area and stayed at the barricaded doors for hours, yelling, "Come out here, Robinson, you son of a bitch. We're gonna get you!" Luckily, several players on the Royals team remained with him until the crowd gave up and left. Unable to get a taxi, they had to accompany him by bus to his hotel to be sure of his safety.

Though people predicted that after a hot hitting start Jackie's average would begin to fall, he kept up the pace. He also continued his prowess as a base stealer. And after a shaky start at second base, he had a streak of seventy-nine games played without committing an error. He became very good as a pivot man in making double plays.

Wherever the Royals played, the presence of Jackie brought out large crowds. Attendance records were being broken in Montreal and on the road. Even in Baltimore, where a close play always threatened to bring on an ugly scene, near record crowds attended the games with Montreal. Many blacks were excited by the presence of one of their own for the first time in organized baseball. As for the whites, if some came to boo, many more wanted to see excellent baseball and sparkling baserunning, especially Jackie's exciting trademark of taking a long lead off third base and looking to steal home. A good number of those who came to jeer stayed to cheer. His style of play made a lot of converts.

The African-American press followed his every move. A black organization called him one of the ten greatest Negroes of the age. Jackie was no less a celebrity in Canada. He was besieged there by well-wishers and autograph hounds wherever he went. If among blacks Jackie became as important as Joe Louis, among Canadians he became almost as important as the ice hockey star, Maurice "the Rocket" Richard, the greatest sports hero of the day in Canada.

Many things contributed to Jackie's rousing success. First and foremost was his superb baseball performance. Hardly less important was his character. His combination of courage, intelligence, integrity, determination, and confidence was unique. He had the self-mastery to control his temper, at least in the first years. Important too was Rickey's support and the appreciation of the hometown fans. Jackie was also carried along by the realization that this was something bigger than just his success. How he did mattered to many people, black and white; it mattered to America itself and its own ideals.

The Montreal team that year proved to be one of the greatest in minor league history. It was a powerhouse, averaging seven runs a game, stealing many bases, and batting almost .300 as a team. It ran away from the rest of the league and clinched the pennant very early. Having a black man on the team not only did not ruin things but actually helped.

Jackie looked as if he performed effortlessly, but he felt himself under tremendous pressure. Always there was the awareness that if he failed, blacks would not get another chance for years. Near the end of the season, Jackie found himself worn out. He could not sleep, and felt nauseated. A doctor, saying that Jackie was near a nervous breakdown, prescribed a period of rest. Jackie tried that but after only two days he was back in the ballpark. He was leading the league in batting, and he feared that a long absence might be seen as an attempt to preserve his high average and win the batting crown by default.

The other black player, Johnny Wright, was unable to bear up under the pressure. He was eventually let go. Another black pitcher brought up to replace him did no better. In July he too was released; but Jackie had established himself as an accepted member of the team. No replacement was needed or brought up. He was on his own.

All in all, it was an outstanding season for anyone at any time. Jackie won the batting title with a formidable .349 average and the fielding title at second base with a .985 percentage of errorless plays. He was also the league leader in runs scored (113) and second in stolen bases (42). He even had sixty-six runs batted in, which was unusually high for someone batting second in the lineup. He was an all-around baseball star. Though still in the minors, he was already better than almost all major league second basemen. His bunting and base-stealing skills reminded observers of the great Ty Cobb. The manager of the Jersey City team said that Jackie bunted better than Cobb had and that he would love to have nine Jackie Robinsons on his team.

That these sensational statistics were put together not by a veteran but by someone breaking into organized baseball, someone carrying a unique burden of responsibility in an unfamiliar environment and facing harassment, cursing, and hatred, turned an outstanding year into an amazing one. Judged in that light, though other players might have better statistics (and very few did!), Jackie was putting on, as someone wrote, "the greatest performance anywhere in sports." It no longer was just spectacular baseball but human interest drama. That year put Jackie among the heroes of history.

The Brooklyn Dodgers were in a tight race with the St. Louis Cardinals, and the logical thing was to bring Jackie up to the majors to help out the parent club. This was logical, but not wise. Rickey resisted the temptation and the pressure for many reasons. Montreal should have the benefit of Jackie's talents in the play-offs and the Little World Series. Jackie needed a full season of preparation and maturing at one place. Rickey himself needed the winter and the spring to carefully prepare the Dodgers and the major leagues for the advent of the first black player. It would be foolish to ruin everything by moving too fast.

After winning the pennant by nineteen-and-a-half

games, the Royals easily defeated Newark and Syracuse in the play-offs. Next they entered the Little World Series against the Louisville, Kentucky, Colonels, the winners of the American Association (also Class AAA). A lot had happened since Jackie first played in Baltimore. He thought he no longer had to prove himself in the South.

On opening day of the series in Louisville, when his name was announced as part of the lineup, he was roundly booed. He was called all the usual names by the fans. Although Montreal won the first game, Jackie performed poorly at the plate. The booing became stronger in the second game. Louisville won the next two games, and Jackie had one hit in eleven at bats in the three games.

In baseball, as in so much else, you are only as good as your last game. So, despite his tremendous season, the Little World Series became a new test of Jackie's ability to handle abuse and pressure. He had to prove himself all over again.

He was trapped in a vicious circle. The crowd was down on him. He slumped at bat, and the crowd got worse as a result. This in turn lowered his morale and play. His every move brought forth a flood of vicious abuse. He had faced nothing like it before.

Luckily, the teams moved to Montreal for the rest of the series. The Canadian fans did not take lightly the treatment their new hero had received from Louisville fans. They now in turn booed the Louisville players, one by one.

In game four, the first at Montreal, Louisville jumped off to a 4–0 lead and came into the ninth inning still ahead, 5–3. The first four Royals walked, making it 5–4 and bringing Jackie, who had been the second batter in the inning, to third base. With no runner ahead of him, he could show his ability. As usual, he took a long lead, threatening to run either home or back to third. This, as usual, distracted pitcher and catcher. The pitcher tried to pick him off but his throw was wild and the ball went into left field. Jackie came easily home to tie the game.

In the tenth inning, with Montreal men on base, Louisville walked a batter intentionally in order to face Jackie, whose batting had slumped in the series. After taking a curve for a strike, Jackie swung at a fastball for a hit and the game-winning run.

In the fifth game, Jackie hit a double and a triple; he scored both times. In the sixth game, he got two of his team's six hits and started two double plays that ended Louisville rallies, including one in the ninth inning. Montreal won the game, 2–0, and won the Little World Series. Having come out of his slump, Jackie ended the series with a .400 average. He had the special satisfaction of scoring the winning run of the last game.

After the game, manager Hopper came up to Jackie before leaving for Mississippi, shook his hand, and said, "Jackie, you're a great ballplayer and a fine gentleman. It's been wonderful having you on the team. I'd sure like to have you back on the Royals next spring. I hope Mr. Rickey won't call you up." To

Rickey, Hopper said, "You don't have to worry none about that boy. He's the greatest competitor I ever saw, and what's more, he's a gentleman."

Thousands of cheering Canadian fans swarmed around Jackie. They tried to touch him or rip off pieces of his clothing. They hoisted him to their shoulders and carried him around the ballpark. Having a plane to catch, Jackie finally managed with great difficulty to get free. "It was," a sportswriter noted, "probably the only day in history that a black man ran from a white mob with love instead of lynching on its mind."

9

THE TORRENTS OF SPRING

(1947)

A few weeks after the thrill of winning the Little World Series, Jackie had an entirely different kind of thrill. Rachel gave birth to their first child, Jack Junior, in November 1946. Parents and child spent the winter in Los Angeles, with Rachel's mother.

They wondered, as did just about every sports-conscious American, whether Jackie would make it to the majors in the upcoming season. It was a big topic of conversation. In the newspapers, as someone said, Jackie's name appeared almost as often as President Truman's. He remained on the Montreal roster and might be sent back there in 1947. Some people, especially black journalists who had been through fake tryouts, still wondered if Rickey was playing a trick.

Jackie's coming to baseball made race a central issue in America in a way that had not happened since the Civil War. In early 1947 a heated meeting of the major league owners was held in New York. Rickey outlined his plan to bring Jackie up to the majors. They pleaded with him not to go through with it.

When the matter was put to a vote, everyone voted against Rickey. He angrily walked out of the meeting. As far as he was concerned, the matter was closed. If they feared riots in ballparks should Jackie be brought up, he feared riots in Harlem if Jackie were not. Rickey talked to Commissioner Chandler, who indicated he would not take a public stand either way. The next move was therefore up to Rickey and Jackie.

Ever the thorough planner, Rickey wanted to prepare the black community for the big move. In early February 1947 he met with prominent blacks—doctors, lawyers, clergymen, journalists, businessmen—and asked for cooperation. He hoped that black fans would repress the natural wish to strike back when they heard white fans at the ballpark call Jackie the inevitable "nigger" and worse. He hoped that the black press would not use Jackie's likely success as an example of the triumph of one race over another or of one political "ism" over another.

What he wanted, above all, was that blacks control their understandable desire to honor Jackie with parades, banquets, and "Jackie Robinson Days." Such functions would add to Jackie's burdens, distract him from baseball, and cause jealousy among his white teammates. Not the least concern, Rickey said, was his fear that too many dinners would make Jackie overweight.

To prevent a repetition of the run-ins with the officials in segregated Florida, Rickey moved Dodger spring training to Havana, Cuba. There the society was integrated, as were the teams the Dodgers would play in exhibition games. This would teach Dodger players something about racial harmony and talented blacks.

Jackie went to Havana in late January 1947 as nervous as he had been the previous year. Money shortages and the presence of a baby forced Rachel to remain behind in California during spring training. Jackie would not, however, be the only black, as he had been in the last half of the previous season. Three others, including the soon-to-be-famous Roy Campanella and Don Newcombe, had been assigned to Montreal.

Jackie was disappointed to find that the four blacks were being separated from the white players. They would be in a hotel far from either the Dodgers or Royals teams. Dodger officials had taken the trouble to leave Florida for Cuba and still blacks were being segregated! The segregation turned out to be the work of the Dodger management, not of the Cubans. Jackie was angry, but Rickey had wanted to move one step at a time. He wanted to prevent any incidents among the players that could ruin the entire experiment. Reluctantly Jackie had to go along.

Rickey's complex strategy required another move that irritated Jackie. He was a shortstop by training who had played second base at Montreal. Brooklyn, though, was blessed with two of the best players in the league at those positions, Pee Wee Reese and Eddie Stanky. To have one of these two popular players removed from his position to make way for Jackie would be another way to stir up racial tension on the team and among white fans. It would suggest that skin color rather than talent had determined the choice.

Luckily, first base was open. The Dodgers needed a good player there. Rickey wanted the versatile Jackie to be broken in at first base. Also, at first base Jackie was less likely to be deliberately spiked by sliding runners. This was a setback for Jackie. At a time when so many other pressures were on him, he had to learn a new position well enough to make the team. Moreover, he developed a bad back and a sore toe. The injuries made getting used to first base play, with its frequent bending, stretching, and quick moves, even harder.

Jackie was unaware of one of the biggest problems facing Rickey then, the backfiring of a careful plan involving Jackie's promotion to the majors. Normally a player who performs well in a Class AAA league is given a chance to try out for the major league team, especially if he wins the batting title, as Jackie had. Rickey, instead, kept Jackie on the Montreal roster.

Rickey believed that a better way to handle the Jackie Robinson case was to let the Dodgers and the Royals play each other in a lot of exhibition games. During these games, Jackie's great talent would make itself clear to everyone. The Dodger players, eager to win and to collect the extra money of World Series play, would demand that Jackie be promoted. The New York press and its readers would join in the demand. This would make it look as if Rickey were only responding to the pressure from the players and the press for a talented individual rather than imposing a black man on them against their wishes.

In preparation for the exhibition games against the Dodgers, Rickey therefore told Jackie to forget the successes of the Montreal year, for this was the real beginning. Jackie was to get on base by any means he could and then run wild on the base paths. He was to put on the show only he could.

This plan sounded smart on paper but had little to do with the real world. For one thing, Jackie was plagued with early spring training injuries. Though he did bat over .500 in exhibition games, he had trouble adjusting to first base. More important, the plan ignored the fact that, for things to happen the way Rickey wanted, the ballplayers also had to be in on the larger picture. The fact is, most players were (and are) mainly concerned with their own individual future. They were so busy trying to make it themselves that they could not worry over whether Jackie would be good for the team.

The biggest flaw in Rickey's plan was that he thought that Jackie's terrific breakthrough at Montreal had settled the race question. Nothing of the sort was true. At this stage, skin color still mattered more to Dodger players than winning. Instead of the Dodgers petitioning Rickey for Jackie to come on board, the exact opposite started to happen.

The Dodgers, like most major league teams, had a sizable number of Southerners on the roster. These players had been brought up in a society that taught them that black people were born inferior, lazy, and disease-ridden. To play on the same team with a black was a loss of honor. To be near a black in a locker room was to risk being infected. That is why otherwise decent, gentle, civilized men like Dixie Walker from Alabama, Pee Wee Reese from Kentucky, and broadcaster Red Barber from Mississippi and Florida were outraged by the arrival of Jackie.

Given their background, the wonder is not their initially hostile reaction but rather the speed with which they were able to overcome a lifetime of conditioning, the ease with which they came to accept Jackie and to appreciate his skills. In their own small ways, they played heroic roles in the story, along with Rickey. But it took all of Jackie's talent and character to open their eyes.

That was later, though. Right now, the leader of the Southerners was Dixie Walker, one of the most popular and valuable players in team history. When Jackie first signed with Montreal, Walker let it be known that if the black man came up to the Dodgers, he would stay home and paint his house that summer. Now in 1947 Walker started circulating a petition that said that those who signed would not play on any team that had Jackie on it.

Walker managed to get most of the other Southerners, and one Northerner, to sign it. The petition drive lost some of its momentum when Pee Wee Reese, a fellow Southerner and another team leader, said that he had a family to support and that he had no choice but to play ball.

One of those asked to sign was Kirby Higbe, a

colorful character and a successful pitcher from South Carolina. Higbe was in a dilemma between being a loyal Southerner or a loyal Dodger. Drinking in a bar, he said to a Dodger official who happened to be there, "Ol' Hig jest cain't do it. Ol' Hig jest cain't be a part of it." The official, taken aback, pumped the whole story out of Higbe. He then rushed out to inform the other Dodger officials.

When the hot-tempered Brooklyn manager, Leo Durocher, got wind of the petition, he felt he had to act hard and fast. If the petition drive went any further, battle lines would be drawn and the club would be split.

Durocher jumped out of bed and woke up the coaches. He had them gather all the players at once. Still in his pajamas, he used a large empty hotel kitchen as a meeting hall. The players entered, in various stages of undress, yawning, rubbing their eyes, finding seats on chopping blocks and counters, leaning against refrigerators and stoves.

Durocher made a speech in which he said things like, "Boys, you know what you can do with that petition. . . . If this guy is good enough to play on this ball club, he is going to play on this ball club, and he is going to play for *me. I'm* the manager of this club, and I'm interested in one thing: winning. . . . This guy is going to win the pennant for us. He's going to put money in your pockets. . . . The meeting is over."

The next day was Rickey's turn. Though he liked to move carefully, he realized that this was a critical moment that required lightning speed. As he later explained, when the law is being violated, a "reasonable" show of force is needed to control things. Rickey now called in the key players individually and laid down the law. He was angry over the petition. He insisted that no word leak out to the press.

One of the players was defiant, and they got into a shouting match. The player said that he would just as soon be traded as play with a black man. Rickey exploded: "Then I may accommodate you, sir!"

Most important, Rickey managed to keep the story from surfacing until it had become a historical footnote. Had it gotten into the newspapers, it would have made Jackie's position very difficult. Had Jackie known of the incident, it might have demoralized him further.

Jackie was having a hard enough time as it was. He had to master the new fielding position. He was having stomach problems and had to miss a few games; a playing injury removed him from some others. Manager Durocher's absence for a while for personal reasons introduced more uncertainty about Jackie's status. Montreal manager Hopper added to the tension by demanding to know for certain if Jackie was going to Brooklyn so that he could try out other players at second base for Montreal.

Jackie met the crisis head on. Though his fielding was less than perfect, his batting was hot. In seven exhibition games between the Dodgers and the Royals, he was the best player of both teams. Yet he was still on the Royals' roster rather than the Dodgers', and his future remained uncertain.

Spring training was drawing to an end. The whole sports world, the whole black community, and a good part of American society were wondering if Jackie would be brought up to the Brooklyn Dodgers. Because the plan to have the Dodger players demand Jackie had failed, the ever-cunning Rickey developed another maneuver. On April 9 and 10, shortly before the season began, the Dodgers and the Royals were to play exhibition games in Ebbets Field, Brooklyn. Rickey instructed Durocher to casually mention to the press that Brooklyn needed only a first baseman to win the pennant, that Jackie was the best prospect for that position, and that he, Durocher, was pressing Mr. Rickey to give Jackie to Brooklyn. So Jackie would be brought up, if not as a result of Dodger player insistence, at least as a result of the Dodger manager's insistence.

It seemed like another fine idea, but it too flopped. On April 9, the very day that Durocher was to make his announcement to the press, Commissioner Chandler, who knew nothing about Rickey's latest plan, suspended Durocher for a year for "conduct detrimental to baseball."

The story of the first black man's entry into organized baseball had become by accident tangled up with another tale that reached a climax at about the same time. Branch Rickey had been feuding with a former apprentice of his, Lee MacPhail, who was then president of the New York Yankees. The feud took a new turn when Rickey hired Durocher from the Cardinals to be the Dodger manager.

Commissioner Chandler had ordered Durocher, often in trouble over his gambling, to avoid all gamblers. During a spring training game several of the gamblers well known to Durocher were seated in MacPhail's box. Rickey, eager to protect Durocher, complained to the press about the commissioner's double standard. Chandler felt that he had to do something dramatic against gambling. He was not willing, though, to hurt MacPhail, who had been instrumental in having him appointed commissioner. He instead suspended Durocher, even though the Dodger manager had kept his word and stayed away from gamblers.

It was nationwide news. Never had a manager been suspended for a whole year. A great debate raged over the justice of the move. Chandler ordered all parties not to talk about the case. Some journalists said that poor Durocher had merely gotten caught in the cross fire between Rickey and MacPhail. That did not matter. Durocher—the man upon whom Rickey had depended to make the "request" for Jackie; the man from Massachusetts who could not care less about a player's color as long as the player helped win games; the man who would do everything possible to make Jackie at home with the Dodgers and who would fight for him—was gone. So was Rickey's latest plan for breaking the color line in the majors.

The opening of the baseball season was a few days away. A decision had to be made about Jackie. The Dodgers, the team that was supposed to rival the New York Yankees and Giants, suddenly had no manager. Jackie had no sponsor in the clubhouse and the dugout.

The players were in disarray, everything was in confusion, and Rickey's strategy seemed to be in the dust.

Rickey had to act fast. He undertook a quick search for a replacement manager. Without the right replacement for Durocher, the experiment could fail. On the very next day, April 10, the Dodgers and the Royals played another spring exhibition game. In the sixth inning, with a Royal on base, Jackie came to bat. He tried to bunt but popped up, and the runner was easily caught off base. At the moment that Jackie hit into the double play, a Brooklyn official handed out a short press release to the journalists in the press box:

> Brooklyn announces the purchase of the contract of Jack Roosevelt Robinson from Montreal. He will report immediately.
>
> Branch Rickey

The phones were jammed, radio programs were interrupted, headlines screamed—a sports story dominated the media and entered the history books. This, while the nation, or at least the part of it called Brooklyn, was still reeling from the previous day's suspension of Durocher.

The color line was officially broken at last. Yet there was something anticlimactic about the story. Not only had it been looked forward to for one and a half years, but it was overshadowed by the surprising Durocher development. Coming in the middle of the explosion over the commissioner's action, the entry of a black man into the major leagues was, as someone put it, like a "whisper in a whirlwind." Maybe the Durocher fiasco even helped by taking some of the pressure and attention from Jackie.

For a Dodgers team already riled up, it was a double punch. To the uncertainties of beginning the baseball season without a manager was abruptly added the prospect of playing alongside a black man. No one was around to monitor such an unprecedented and delicate situation in the clubhouse and the dugout. Durocher was sorely missed.

On April 10 Jackie quietly moved his belongings across the field, from the Royals' dressing room to the Dodgers'. He was given number 42.

Nineteen forty-seven was proving to be a wild year in baseball.

10

A MONTH IN HELL
(April-May 1947)

The twenty-eight-year-old Jackie Robinson was pretty old for a rookie. On the other hand, his experience and maturity helped him cope. He thought that after all the turbulence in the Montreal season, coming to the Dodgers would be a cinch. Certainly his first series of Dodger games went without a hitch or extra excitement.

Jackie the Dodger immediately began to draw large crowds. Many more black fans than in past years attended. There was no sign of racial tension and, as Rickey had requested, there was no big fuss made in the black community. The spring training season ended with a series of exhibition games against the Yankees. The Dodgers were temporarily managed by one of the coaches. Jackie played first base and batted second in the order. He handled himself well in the field and, though hitless, he did bat in three runs.

Then came opening day. The Brooklyn crowds, the opposing players, and his new teammates were friendly, cool, or just curious. Everyone took the opening day game in stride. No special fuss was made over the desegregation of baseball. When Jackie first came to bat, he grounded out to shortstop. It was a close call at first base. Jackie was tempted to argue the call, as he would have in the Negro league, but his special agreement with Rickey prevented that.

As a hitter, Jackie started out far less spectacularly than he had in his debut game with Montreal. Facing one of the best pitchers in the league, Johnny Sain, he grounded out, flied out, hit into a double play, and got on base on an error and scored. But he played first base as though it had always been his position.

In the second game, he was still nervous and swinging wildly. In fact he was hitless in his first twenty times at bat. The slump affected his morale. Perhaps Bob Feller had been right when he said that Jackie could not hit major league pitching.

Rickey had in the meantime found a replacement for Durocher. Burt "Barney" Shotton was a soft-spoken, fatherly type. It could be that not having the hard-talking Durocher on hand to fight for the first black player was a blessing in disguise. Shotton was a man of few words, and he never went out onto the playing field. His quiet style was better suited for the stormy days ahead than was Durocher's tendency to stir up trouble everywhere with his hot temper and his big mouth. At any rate, Jackie was grateful to the new manager for having faith in him during the early-season slump.

Jackie impressed the journalists by the way he spoke only when spoken to, answered all questions quietly and intelligently, and did not try to force himself on anyone. That would be his style all season long. That style, though, had yet to be tested by adversity. After the uneventful series with Boston and New York came the first of many crises that summer.

The Philadelphia Phillies were scheduled to play in Brooklyn. The president of the Phillies phoned Rickey to say that his team would not play if Jackie was on the field. Rickey answered that that would be just fine with him because, according to the rule book, it would mean three Dodger victories by forfeit. So the Phillies, their bluff called, played.

Their manager was Ben Chapman, a rough customer hailing from Alabama. He had been known in prior years to make anti-Semitic remarks to fans in the stands. When Jackie came to bat in the first inning, the entire Phillies bench, under orders from Chapman, started a chorus of racist and obscene remarks. "Hey, nigger, why don't you go back to the cotton field where you belong?" was one of the milder, printable ones.

"Bench jockeying," hurling insulting remarks and names at players, especially rookies, is part of baseball. It is often done for laughs. But now with Jackie it was racist, angry, and ugly. The Phillies continued it throughout the game.

At first Jackie was stunned. Then he became angry. He felt a strong urge to go over to the bench, grab one of the loudest players, and punch him just as hard as he could. He says in his autobiography that for one long minute he thought, "To hell with Mr. Rickey's noble experiment!" With great effort Jackie did restrain himself.

That was one of the worst days of Jackie's life. He came closer to cracking then than on any other day. To have this Deep South hatred flare up in New York City and on a northern team was shocking. To be pressured later by team officials to take a photo of a pretended "reconciliation" with Chapman was one of the hardest things he ever had to do.

Yet that incident proved to be in some ways a turning point. Suddenly the world knew what Jackie was up against, and he had many well-wishers. Certainly the hometown fans were with him. If Montreal had been a good place in which a black man could enter organized baseball, Brooklyn was equally good for an entry into the major leagues. The large immigrant population of Irish, Italians, Jews, and Scandinavians readily identified with one man's attempt to make his way, in the face of prejudice, into the American establishment. As one owner said, "If Jackie Robinson was the ideal man to break the color line, Brooklyn was the ideal place."

Moreover, the sportswriters had heard the abuse, and they came down hard on Chapman and his team. They demanded that the commissioner act. He did; he warned the Phillies' owner that that sort of thing had no place in baseball and had better stop. Chapman was forced to explain himself to black reporters. The Phillies stopped their racial slurs. Instead they resorted to more subtle stuff: They pointed their bats at Jackie and made machine-gun-like sounds.

More importantly, the incident vindicated Rickey's confidence that the Dodgers would back their beleaguered black teammate. By the time of the third game against the Phillies, Eddie Stanky, who had been one of the anti-Jackie group in the days of the petition, yelled out, "Listen, you yellow-bellied cowards, why don't you holler at somebody who can answer back?" Dixie Walker, of all people, backed Stanky in defending the black man. Jackie, though claiming that the jockeying had not gotten to him, greatly appreciated the help he now received from his teammates. Besides, he got his revenge through baseball. In one of the games he singled, stole second, went to third on a wild throw, and scored on a hit. That proved to be the only run in the game.

From then on, Stanky went out of his way to be helpful to Jackie, giving him fielding tips and encouraging him. Walker eventually did the same. His advice on batting stances and hitting strategy later helped bring Jackie out of his slump. Chapman had ironically aided Jackie by creating sympathy for him among the Dodgers and in the baseball world. Others' bigotry had glued together a team that had been split over the matter of race.

Now the hunting season on Jackie began in earnest. He was hit by pitches more often than any other player, and he was the target of base runners. As a fielder, he quickly learned to tag first base faster than any player in history to avoid being spiked. In the face of all the provocation he managed to keep quiet, as he had promised. He got his revenge instead with the mayhem he caused on the base paths.

Off the playing field, life was hardly much easier. Jackie's mail was filled with hate letters, with threats to kill him, to assault his wife, to kidnap his baby son. On May 9 Jackie turned over letters with death threats to the press. On that same day, a story appeared in a New York newspaper that the St. Louis Cardinals, at that time the team in the southernmost city in the major leagues, had allegedly planned a protest strike three days earlier, on the day of the first Dodger visit, May 6. They were going to try to start a leaguewide movement to force Jackie out of baseball.

It eventually turned out that the story was an exaggeration. Some players had talked about it, but none had been able to organize anything. At the time the story came out, however, things looked ominous. It was also reported that National League president Ford Frick, who had once been against blacks entering organized baseball, had threatened to suspend from baseball any player participating in anything like a strike.

The story caused another sensation in a year of baseball sensations. Many newspapers were awakened to the extent of racism in baseball, and the press came down hard on the Cardinal players.

Resentment against Jackie was heard on every team, but once the rumored St. Louis strike threat was apparently put down, other teams fell in line. The Chicago Cubs management, with the St. Louis case as a precedent, abruptly stopped their team from doing anything. Various other baseball front offices took precautions and issued warnings to their teams. President Frick's hard line and the publicity given the story helped save the integrity of baseball. After St. Louis, things became a little easier for Jackie. A major hurdle had been overcome.

Both ugly incidents actually worked in Jackie's favor. Racist words were publicly condemned. The officials, the newspapers, and the public were shown to be with Jackie, not with the racists. There were many well-wishers out there. Whether Jackie would remain in the majors was up to him, not to the haters.

At the beginning, life with his Dodger teammates was not any easier for Jackie. They knew that he was there and that they would have to learn to play with him. That is not the same as being friendly. His roommate on the road was a black reporter, not a teammate. In a segregated city like St. Louis, he had to room in town with a black family and could be with the Dodgers only on the field and in the clubhouse.

He did not force himself on the players. He spoke only when spoken to. He ate with others only when invited to do so. He was at first reluctant to shower with the other players, knowing how whites, especially Southern ones, feared catching diseases from blacks in shower rooms. He had to keep busy on train rides so as to avoid getting caught up in card games with the players, where so many things could go wrong.

He had to know his place. When he was on base

and Walker hit a home run, as happened three times that year, Jackie could not follow the baseball custom of waiting at home plate to shake Walker's hand. Walker might refuse to do so. And besides any personal distaste Walker might have, what would the South think of one of its sons shaking hands with a black man in front of thousands of people? Walker had a sporting goods store back home to worry about, and Southerners could be unforgiving that way. No wonder that one journalist described Jackie as "the loneliest man in baseball."

Jackie had to put up quietly with everyday insults, sometimes unintended ones. When he finally got to play card games with his teammates, there was the time a Southern player complained of bad luck. The Southerner explained that back home in Georgia, whenever he ran into bad luck at cards, he would go out and rub himself against the "biggest, blackest nigger woman" he could find. The player then rubbed Jackie's head.

A terrible silence descended on everyone. All eyes turned to Jackie, who was smoldering inside. It took all of Jackie's willpower to keep from reacting violently. Finally, to everyone's relief, Jackie turned to the dealer and said simply, "Deal the cards."

After the St. Louis incident, things became easier, but not easy. Many were the times when an umpire made a wrong call or an opposing player made extra hard body contact or a pitcher threw a beanball. Always Jackie had to swallow and take it, even at the risk of looking like a coward. He knew that he was part of an experiment and that the larger scheme, the big picture, was more important than his personal feelings. Still, the inner Jackie was hurting.

In one run-in with a Chicago Cub, when the player kicked Jackie, he instinctively raised his fist to retaliate, but just in time held back. In a series with the St. Louis Cardinals during a struggle for first place, Jackie was spiked by a different player in each of two games. Again the Dodgers rallied to Jackie's defense and angrily threatened retaliation. Even Hugh Casey of Georgia came out of the dugout to protest the Cardinals' playing.

In another series Cardinals catcher Joe Garagiola made a racial slur. Jackie exploded and the two had to be held back. In response, Jackie then hit a two-run homer to win the game, 4–3.

Life at home wasn't ideal either. His salary of $5,000 a year was the official major league minimum. It was barely enough to live on with a family. Though he drew vast crowds, he could not by law receive any increases or bonuses during the season. A white player with Jackie's fame and drawing power would have been able to pick up many times that amount in commercial endorsements and media appearances. Part of Rickey's careful planning, however, was not to cheapen Jackie's image. He wanted Jackie in the public eye only in connection with baseball.

With extra money not available, Jackie, his wife, and their child were stuck in a single room in a midtown Manhattan hotel, where they had gone when they were waiting to hear whether their destination was Montreal or Brooklyn. There they could not afford to hire a baby-sitter or to dine out together, and had to take turns eating out alone. The best they could do a few weeks into the season was to share an apartment in Brooklyn with a black woman who had a busy social life. That proved to be an awkward arrangement in cramped quarters.

In the middle of all this, Jackie was slumping. He was having trouble hitting the major league curveball. The attention of the outside world, the pressure on him to make good, a sore shoulder, a batting slump, on-field harassment, threats to himself and his family, the absence of good lodgings—that first month in the majors was pure hell for Jackie. Many players, both black and white, teammates and opponents, affirmed then (and later) that neither they nor anyone else could have taken what Jackie did. And they only knew a fraction of what he was going through.

Sometimes he would call home to Pasadena and tell his family in a choking voice, "I can't take it anymore," and he would talk of quitting. He was just letting off steam. His commitment to the black cause, as well as his own self-respect, kept him going. Only a very special sort of man could shut it all out and do what had to be done.

Most of the early black players who came along with or soon after Jackie could not in fact take it and were driven out of baseball by this storm of abuse. But the racial taunts, which he could not respond to, made him play higher-quality ball. Ever the clutch player, he practiced the baseball version of "Don't get mad, get even." They might curse his color all they liked, but he would run them ragged on the bases.

Ben Chapman finally learned his lesson. Toward the end of the season, with Brooklyn in first place and Philadelphia in last, he ordered his players to lay off Jackie. "Don't get him any madder than he is."

11

RICH AND FAMOUS
(May-December 1947)

At the beginning of the season the pressure was greater than it had ever been in Montreal. Jackie started slowly and slumped. When he began stealing bases, things got better. Finally, late in May, Jackie came into his own. The base hits started, and he was so good as a fielder at first base that the two other Dodger first basemen were traded. Even Chapman had to admit that Jackie belonged in the majors. In June he had a streak of twenty-one games in which he got at least one hit. He was batting over .300. He was first or second in the league in stolen bases and runs scored.

As long as the Dodgers felt themselves to be part—or, in the case of the Southerners, victims—of a great experiment in race relations, they were cool to Jackie. When they saw that his playing was going to help them win the pennant, they learned to ignore his skin color. Gradually the team warmed up to him. Rickey's scheming, which had flopped badly in spring training, was finally bearing fruit. It took little more than a month, less time actually than at Montreal, for Jackie to be accepted as a regular. Dixie Walker, who had written a letter to Rickey asking to be traded, asked for the letter back.

Soon Jackie was eating at the same table with the others, participating in bull sessions and card games. By the end of the season, the Dodgers were downright enthusiastic about their black teammate. He had met insults and violence with silence and gained the respect of his teammates. What really won them over was his drive to win; victory in the pennant race meant money in the pocket. He had become more visible as a brilliant player than as a black player. The men on the other teams also began to respect him.

Turning the other cheek succeeded as Rickey had predicted. Integration in baseball began without violence or legislation. Blacks and whites played together and then sat down to eat together. It was a joint enterprise. When a black scored a run, no one questioned the color of the run. Jackie acted out the philosophy of nonviolence of Martin Luther King, Jr., before the future civil rights leader had thought of applying it to the problem of segregation in America. And it worked.

The biggest conquest of all, because he was heard by millions, was Red Barber. The great announcer confessed on the air between innings of a game in May that he had been completely won over by the black man's abilities and courage. This Southerner who now admired Jackie so much said, "I hope he bats 1.000!"

*   *   *

Jackie was changing the face of baseball not only by being the first black man in it but also by the style of play he brought to the game. On the base paths, he put on a great show, speeding or threatening, diving or rocking, dancing or bluffing. He brought back to life the fine old art of stealing which had been perfected by Ty Cobb and buried by a quarter century of home run mania begun by Babe Ruth.

The battle of wits surrounding a stolen base is for lower stakes—only one base, rather than the homer's four bases and its potential for multiple runs—but it can bring more excitement to the playing field. In fact, a home run, by clearing the bases, sometimes nips the fans' excitement, while a stolen base can add momentum. The stolen base is man racing ball and having to make instant decisions about time and space. The home run requires only muscle; the stolen base requires speed, reflexes, cunning, and daring.

Stealing bases was only one item in Jackie's repertoire. Another specialty of his was the rundown. Once he was at first, he took a large lead. Following Rickey's instructions to distract the pitcher, he told the pitcher he was going to steal and dared him to stop him. He took longer leads than anyone else. He went back and forth, back and forth, keeping the fielders uncertain whether he would steal or was bluffing. He had the necessary timing, balance, and agility for this maneuver. He could stop and start unusually fast. He could fake either movement perfectly. He was uncanny in changing directions abruptly. A careful student of a pitcher's movements and defects, he kept one step ahead of the other team's pitcher and fielders. Combined with his unique quickness in going from a standing position to full speed in just a few steps, this made him a terror.

After bluffing a few times, he would take off for second base just as the pitcher threw to the first baseman, who threw to the second baseman and then back to first, and so on. The other infield players—everyone but the hot dog vendors, was the joke—would close in, like a wolf pack, for the kill. But thanks to a bad throw, a dropped ball, or sheer timing by Jackie, more often than not he eluded them all and got safely to second or back to first.

When he reached first, he often could get to second and then third on stolen bases, wild throws, or a balk caused by his distractions. Opposing teams had long meetings on what to do once he got on base. Just as in his youthful playing days at school, the motto became, "Stop Robinson!" The damage this did to the concentration of pitchers and how often it resulted in walks and hits by countless other batters cannot show up in the statistics.

Another specialty of Jackie's was at third base. There he would dance, dare the pitcher, pretend to run home, make it back to third just in time, take a long lead again, balance himself, hands swinging, ready to go either way. Sometimes when the pitcher threw to third, he was off for home. Sometimes the pitcher became so distracted that he balked and Jackie had the satisfaction of trotting home.

In one June game against the Cubs, Jackie ran all the way home from first on a bunt, while the frustrated Cubs simply threw the ball around the infield trying in vain to catch him. Another time, he walked and, while the catcher argued with the umpire over the call, went right on to second. In a game with Pittsburgh, Jackie was on third, and the pitcher chased him back to base with several tosses. As the pitcher then started to wind up, Jackie stole home to win the game, 3–2. The Pittsburgh crowd went as wild as if he were one of their own team's players. For turning a game around or bringing a crowd to their feet, there was no one like him. This was not ordinary baseball. It was athletic excellence. It was show business at its finest.

The team worked smoothly. Stanky and Jackie, the first two batters, were the "table setters," that is, the men whose job it was to get on base by any means. Stanky was a master at getting walks, and Jackie was a master bunter, setting the stage for the high-powered bats of Reiser and Walker. Often Jackie was able to outrun a bunt and give the sluggers more runners to bring home. Or he singled and sent Stanky to third.

Jackie was a spark plug, inspiring his team and confusing the opposition. He was usually at the heart of any rally. He had a knack for shining in critical situations and before large crowds. Intense and competitive, he played to win. He could beat the other team in many different ways—with a bunt or a line-drive hit or an extra-base hit or a home run or a stolen base or a great fielding play or a well-turned double play. As teammate and slugger Duke Snider put it,

Jackie made the Dodgers closer by his suffering and made them better by his ability.

The Dodgers got into first place in July and remained there. In September Jackie went on a hitting streak that helped win the pennant for Brooklyn. A hot second half of the season brought his season average to .297, rare for a rookie. Finally Rickey relaxed his strict rules. He allowed the fans to hold a Jackie Robinson Day. It happened to come the day after the Dodgers clinched the pennant. That was poetic justice. Among the many who honored Jackie was Dixie Walker. The legendary black dancer Bill "Bojangles" Robinson said that he had lived to see a "Ty Cobb in Technicolor." Since Ty Cobb was a racist, this was yet more poetic justice. A few days later, a ticker tape parade was held in Brooklyn for all the Dodgers, with some half million people in attendance. Walker and Jackie, among others, spoke.

Jackie's statistics for the year were impressive. He appeared in more games than any other Dodger (151 out of 154), despite injuries caused by spiking and brushback pitches. He led his team in runs scored (125) and stolen bases (29, twice as many as anyone else in the league). He got 174 hits, 14 more than Dixie Walker. His 12 home runs tied Reese for the team lead. He set a new record with 28 sacrifice hits. All this was accomplished by someone under death threats and other daily harassments.

The *Sporting News*, which had long opposed letting blacks into baseball, selected Jackie as the first recipient of the Rookie of the Year award. Dixie Walker, the leader of the petition conspiracy, said, "No other ballplayer on this club has done more to put the Dodgers up in the race than Robinson has." Jackie had proved the black man's right to a place in baseball. A lot of experts had been shown to be wrong.

In one respect Jackie became an unqualified success very early. Some club owners had been against breaking the color line for fear of losing money, but the coming of Jackie had the opposite effect. Just as it had in the minor league, money was pouring in. The major league games had had few black spectators. Now blacks came from everywhere to see the Dodgers. Whites also came in droves.

They were drawn not just by the uniqueness of skin color. Other black players who soon followed did not have such an attraction. They were drawn rather by the daring and the showmanship of one of the most exciting players of all time. Tickets were often being scalped as if for the World Series. Attendance records at home and on the road were being broken. With the whole country watching him, Jackie was more of an attraction than any player in history except Babe Ruth.

What Jackie did, and the attendance he drew, helped the other owners revise their thinking. Jackie could well be proud to have opened the door for others. By July, the head of the Cleveland Indians, saying that Jackie "has proved to be a real big leaguer," signed up Larry Doby from the Negro League and put him on the Indians roster without even minor league seasoning. The American League was thus integrated too. The pressures and the attention were no longer on an isolated Jackie. He need not feel that if he failed, the black cause would fail. In fact, Rickey deliberately did not try to gobble up all the black talent available but saw that it was in baseball's interest to have capable blacks on other teams.

As the southernmost city in baseball, St. Louis seemed the least likely to hire black players; but the St. Louis Browns were last in the standings and attendance. The team had to do something drastic and signed up two black players. But, when the two did not make it as big league athletes, the black press had to remind its readers that not all black players can be "a Robinson." In fact, at the end of 1947, only Jackie *had* succeeded. He was unique.

The World Series was enough to make anyone giddy, especially a rookie, especially the first black in baseball, especially in cavernous, legendary Yankee Stadium with its capacity of 73,000. Not Jackie, though. "It can't be any more nerve-racking," he said to the press, "than that St. Louis series. After that, nothing can seem too important." That he was the first African American to play in a World Series no longer mattered. The novelty of a black man being in baseball had worn off.

The Dodgers now again faced the hated Yankees in what turned out to be one of the most exciting World Series in history. Jackie put on a fine show. At bat, he was 7 for 27 (.259), tying Reese for the most Dodger hits. He stole only three bases, but every time he got on base, he caused confusion in Yankee ranks.

Yogi Berra, the rookie catcher, had come up to the Yankees from Newark at the same time that Jackie had come up to the Dodgers from Montreal. The catcher therefore thought that he knew Jackie's work from that 1946 season in the International League. He told reporters that Jackie had not stolen a base against him in that year in the minors and would not now in the series. The reporters, of course, rushed to tell Jackie that. He smiled. "We'll see about that."

In the first inning of the first game, Jackie walked and put on one of his famous baserunning shows. He immediately took off for second base. Berra's throw was hurried and poor. Walker's single brought Jackie home. Later he said, "I wish Berra was catching in the National League. I'd steal sixty bases." In his second at bat, Jackie walked again, this time so distracting the pitcher with his dance that he was awarded second on a balk. Before the Series was over, Berra was only too glad to be relieved of catching duties.

The Yankees won the first two games, but the Dodgers at home in Brooklyn came back to win 9–7 in the third game, as Jackie got two hits. In the fifth game he knocked in a run. Unfortunately the Yankees won the seventh and deciding game.

In the defeated team's locker room, there was a consolation of sorts, if the players were aware of it. They had the distinction of being the team to have broken the color barrier for baseball, and for other sports as well. Many of the Dodgers, as they were leaving for home, told Jackie that he was a "fine man" as well as "one hell of a ballplayer."

Few athletes had ever known a year so full of highs and lows and off-the-field fireworks. Jackie had come through it all intact. He was now one very famous athlete. He had established a place for blacks in the great American game and a place for himself in history. Jackie's first season is like something out of fiction. It is a story out of an America we like to believe really exists. Jackie was not only a great ballplayer but also an American hero, a symbol of black aspirations.

He had become a legend overnight. Near the end of the season, it was announced that he would star in a motion picture about his life. His mother could, after a lifetime of hardships and anxieties, finally stop being a domestic and go into a comfortable and well-earned retirement. He had kept his vow to compensate her for all she had done for her children.

Though at season's end he actually did get a job for a short while as a salesman for an appliance store in Brooklyn, he need not have worried. Acclaim and rewards and money now poured in. He finally received permission from Rickey to make endorsements of products. He was, of course, the first black athlete to do so. Soon there was a veritable industry of Jackie Robinson dolls, caps, jackets, and trinkets.

He went barnstorming. He participated in theatrical tours and vaudeville acts, earning at least $2,500 for each performance. He was free to follow up on the many invitations to banquets. In those days before television, he often was heard on the radio. He wrote, with a ghostwriter, his autobiography. Later he was given the title of editor of a magazine, and under his byline appeared a regular column in a black newspaper. As a result of all these activities, he made more money than almost any other major league player.

He had hardly any time or privacy. Everywhere people flocked to him as to a media superstar, for an autograph, a touch, a piece of his clothing. Mail, the good kind now, poured in. Politicians rushed to be photographed shaking his hand. He won all sorts of awards. He ended up on the cover of *Time* magazine. In one poll, he was voted the second most popular man in America, trailing only singer Bing Crosby.

Even the black community was surprised. It knew and hoped he would be good, but he proved to be better than anyone's expectations. He became a folk hero. Blacks traveled hundreds of miles to see him play. They wore their Sunday best clothes as they sat among more casually dressed whites. Even African Americans indifferent to baseball wanted to know how Jackie had done every day.

Black children suddenly realized that they could make it to the big time. Their hopes and dreams were ignited when he passed through their city or if they read about his success. Future black stars like Lou Brock, Elston Howard, and Hank Aaron have told of how the world opened for them and how they were inspired to higher goals by the news about Jackie. They could make it as baseball players now and perhaps in other ways too. A survey published in the black magazine *Ebony* found Jackie to be one of the ten most significant blacks in American history—and this after only his first year in major league baseball!

That Jackie's achievement went far beyond baseball is brought out by the story told of an old black woman in the rural South who knew little of baseball. She listened to a game on the radio to hear how the great Jackie Robinson was doing. She was shocked to hear the announcer say that Jackie had just stolen a base. She burst out: "They just lyin'. That Jackie Robinson is a nice boy. He wouldn't steal a thing!"

12

THE VETERAN
(1948)

Now that Jackie had finally made the big time and captured everyone's admiration, he found himself sucked into the celebrity circuit. Baseball players get a five-month vacation every year during which they are free to do what they wish. The winter means invitations to banquets, talks to fraternal lodges and college groups, appearances and endorsements, meetings over business deals. For Jackie there were literally thousands of requests for his personal appearance between the seasons of 1947 and 1948.

He followed through on some of them. A winter speaking tour of the South, among other activities, resulted in his frequent exposure to the best Southern cooking in middle-class black homes. Those calories began to pile up. When he showed up for spring training in 1948 he was some twenty to twenty-five pounds overweight.

Leo Durocher, his one-year suspension over, was back as manager. The first thing Durocher remarked on when greeting the newly arrived Jackie was that he had gotten fat. It looked like Jackie was so busy enjoying his success that he did not care about his future in baseball. Jackie's obesity ruined the strategy of the Dodger management. Rickey wanted to put Jackie at his natural position, second base. To that end, Eddie Stanky, the second baseman, had been traded. (Dixie Walker was also gone.) But how could Jackie play a position where more speed was needed if he was out of condition?

Durocher seemed to take it personally. It looked like Jackie stayed in condition for Burt Shotton but not for him. That may explain why Durocher seemed to humiliate Jackie. He treated Jackie as if he were a rookie, forcing him to do special exercises, making him bend and sweat a lot in the tropical heat. The exercises were humiliating because press, teammates, and even rookies were the spectators.

This was the first time that Jackie had received such criticism from anyone on the Dodgers. He was never good at taking criticism. Now he took it personally too; he was angry. Jackie and Durocher did not get on in other ways either. Jackie needed reassurance that he was great. Durocher preferred to chew players out, even those he respected. Screaming at a player was his way of liking and helping him. Jackie could not adjust to that style.

Meanwhile, during the 1948 spring training season, Rickey brought his experiment deeper into the Jim Crow South. After training in the Dominican Republic, the team played in Texas, Oklahoma, and North

Carolina. It was, of course, the first team with a black man on it to play in these states. Yet some city officials had actually asked for the Dodgers, and for Jackie specifically, to appear. As usual by now, fans broke attendance records in order to see the new sensation in sports.

There were the expected death threats and occasional attempts to bar Jackie. Again Durocher, always one to fight for his men, said to local officials that if Jackie did not play, the team would not either. Pee Wee Reese jokingly asked Jackie to stand near someone else on the field. "Because if they shoot and miss, I don't want them to get me."

Despite being Rookie of the Year, a national hero, and a magnet for spectators, in the segregated South Jackie was still a nobody outside the ballpark. Once after a hard game, he had to stay in the bus, hungry and tired, while the rest of the team had a good, leisurely meal in a nice restaurant. Jackie seemed to be close then to walking out on everything. When a team official brought some hamburgers out to the bus, Jackie was so enraged that he would not touch the food.

With Durocher's exercises, Jackie managed to shed some 15 pounds. But he did not get into full shape until June. He performed poorly in the early part of the season. So did the rest of the team, with many of its best players traded, over the hill, or injured. The previous year's pennant winners were actually in last place for some time and had an eight-game losing streak. Durocher, an irritable man to begin with, was boiling mad over what this meant for his reputation as a manager. Shotton had led a divided and confused team into the World Series; Durocher was leading a pennant winner into the cellar.

Rumors abounded. The players were said to dislike the noisy Durocher after having been led by the quiet and successful Shotton. In June there was talk of Durocher being fired. Feeling the heat, the manager experimented more. He put Jackie back at first base for a while and had Rickey bring Roy Campanella up from Montreal. Now Jackie again had a black player as a roommate, this time one who would remain on the team.

Campanella soon became the top catcher. This forced Durocher to make catcher Gil Hodges a first baseman and, in turn, move Robinson back to second base. Duke Snider became the center fielder, and Carl Furillo replaced Dixie Walker in right field. Billy Cox, obtained from Pittsburgh in return for the aging Walker, took over third base, where he became the best fielder at that position in the majors. The great new Dodger team of the future, prepared for by Rickey since 1943, was taking shape.

Time was needed, though, and time was precisely what Durocher had run out of. Brooklyn grew dispirited over its team, attendance dropped, and Rickey was being pressured by the two other owners of the Dodgers to fire the manager. Even though the team was starting to turn around, it was too late.

On July 15 the news came that Durocher had been let go by Brooklyn and hired by their crosstown rivals, the New York Giants. Shotton was returning as manager. Jackie was glad to see him. Coincidentally, Ben Chapman was fired on that same day as Phillies manager.

By this time Jackie, having shed his extra weight, regained his normal playing skill. The timing made it seem as if Jackie gave his all for Shotton, not Durocher. A feud now developed between Jackie and Durocher, especially when the two teams played each other. Durocher, as third base coach, would yell things to Jackie at second base. He put his hands at the side of his head to suggest that Jackie had a swelled head. Jackie in turn answered that Durocher used his wife's perfume. Durocher blew up and called him all sorts of names. They often went at it like that and sometimes almost came to blows. Skin color aside, they were similar in their intensity, competitiveness, and hotheadedness. Admiring Jackie for beating the opposition "a thousand times in a thousand ways," Durocher generously said of Jackie, "He was a Durocher with talent."

A month after Shotton's return, the Dodgers were back in first place. Jackie was coming into his own again; the Dodgers resumed the risk-taking running game of the previous year. Yet they were unable to hold on to first place. The rival Giants, led by Durocher, swept one three-game series. A losing streak in September finished the Dodgers off. They ended up in third place.

Jackie's batting average was almost exactly the same as the previous year: .296. He scored 108 runs and batted in 85. He collected 12 home runs, 22 stolen bases, and 170 hits. At second base, his first year in the majors at that position, he led the league with a fielding average of .983.

More important, in 1948 the novelty of being the first and the only black in the majors had worn off. A highlight of this year was, paradoxically, Jackie's getting thrown out of a game. The Dodger bench was riding an umpire over his call of a pitch. When the umpire issued a warning, Jackie ignored it. The umpire pointed at him and yelled, "You, Robinson! Yer outta the game!" That expulsion meant that he was not getting special treatment because of his color. He was, as a newspaper put it, "just another guy." That had been the goal of the great experiment.

As "just another guy," Jackie could begin to exercise some of his natural leadership qualities. When pitcher Carl Erskine came up to the Dodgers that year, Jackie was a veteran big leaguer on the team, not a black man or "the first black." The no longer shy Jackie took it upon himself to tell Erskine that he had seen him in spring training and knew that he could help the team. Jackie was accurate in his assessment of Erskine's greatness.

He would often tell a promising player that he had Dodger potential. To an aspiring young athlete that could be quite a morale booster. When someone was traded to the Dodgers, Jackie would be the first one to greet him. As more blacks joined the team, Jackie made sure that they did not have lockers together and did not hang around with one another at meals and in the locker room. He urged them to mingle with the white players. This shows the amount of thought he, like his mentor Rickey, put into the integration process, as well as his understanding of psychology. It also shows how he took charge. In later years, his was the locker in the center of the Dodger clubhouse.

The uniqueness of Jackie is shown by the fact that his success in 1946 and 1947 did not cause the walls of segregation to tumble down. That came rather after the 1948 season. The success of Larry Doby with the Cleveland Indians proved that other black ballplayers could match the major leaguers. Jackie had not proved that. He was too special in skills and in drawing power. You could not generalize about the run-of-the-mill black player on the basis of what this exceptional man was able to do.

Jackie as a football
star, 1937–1940
*(Courtesy
Metromedia TV)*

Jackie as a basketball star, 1937–1940
(Courtesy Metromedia TV)

Jackie on the UCLA track-and-field team, 1937–1940
(Courtesy National Baseball Library, Cooperstown, N.Y.)

Jackie during his army service *(Courtesy Bettmann Archive)*

Jackie at Ebbets Field, breaking through the Keep Out barrier on April 10, 1947, an important day in American history *(Courtesy Wide World)*

Jackie breaking into the major leagues as a first baseman in the spring of 1947 at Brooklyn's legendary Ebbets Field *(Courtesy Bettmann Archive)*

Jackie at one of his specialties—stealing home *(Courtesy Wide World)*

Jackie receiving a silver bat from National League president Ford Frick after being both league batting champion (.342) and Most Valuable Player in 1949 (spring 1950) *(Courtesy Bettmann Archive)*

Jackie being inducted into the Baseball Hall of Fame in July 1962. From left to right, the three most influential people in his life: his mentor, Branch Rickey; his wife, Rachel Isum Robinson; and his mother, Mallie McGriff Robinson. *(Courtesy National Baseball Library, Cooperstown, N.Y.)*

13

THE NEW JACKIE ROBINSON
(1949)

In 1949 the time had come to unleash Jackie. The three years (including the one in Montreal) of turning the other cheek for the sake of a higher cause were up. The mission was accomplished. While heroically controlling his inclination to talk up, lash out, strike back, Jackie had proved himself a big league player. Other blacks were making their way into the majors. As a group they were there to stay. The trend could not be reversed, no matter what happened to any one player. A black was no longer a freak or a delicate plant. He had the right to sound off and to err like any human being. He could continue to be a role model, but he didn't have to be a quiet one.

Realizing that the time had come for an "emancipation proclamation," Branch Rickey called Jackie into his office and said, "Jackie, you're on your own now. You've earned the right to be yourself." Rickey knew that Jackie's self-control, while necessary at the beginning, was misunderstood by many in baseball. They could only respect fighting back. They knew courage only in its physical sense. Rickey now eagerly waited for Jackie to show the major leagues "a thing or two."

During the spring training of 1949, Jackie announced, "They better be rough on me this year, because I'm sure gonna be rough on them." He would take nothing from anyone anymore, umpire or player, teammate or opponent. He would fight for his rights. He would take a strong stand against antiblack insults. He would denounce the segregation of ballplayers in the Southern cities that the teams visited. He would be no longer only a silent hero but also a noisy spokesman.

Enjoying the confrontations, he argued with umpires, players, and reporters. From then on, he was as famous for the controversies he got into as for his baseball feats.

Soon after announcing he would be rough, he had a run-in with Chris Van Kuyk, a tall rookie Dodger pitcher from the South, and the two men had to be separated. Jackie's outspokenness was directed as readily to the highest authority as to a rookie. When Commissioner Chandler called him into his office to discuss that incident and Jackie's newly proclaimed boldness, Robinson immediately took the offensive. He asked whether Chandler would have done the same if Ty Cobb had spoken out. Chandler replied that he was worried about a riot breaking out in the ballpark as a result of Jackie's new style. Cobb—Jackie would have to admit—did not present such a problem. Jackie then said that he would not go out looking for trouble but neither would he turn the other cheek. Chandler said he could live with that attitude.

For starters, Jackie had a few scores to settle. There was his old nemesis, Ben Chapman, now a coach with Cincinnati. Once, during practice, Chapman made a remark implying that Jackie was too "delicate." Jackie went over to Chapman and offered to meet him outside the ballpark after the game. No more was heard from Chapman.

The new Jackie was ready to physically challenge pitchers he thought were trying to bean him. That is how he handled Sal "the Barber" Maglie, a Giant who specialized in giving batters a "close shave." After too many close ones from Maglie, Jackie in two separate plays charged hard into the Giants' second baseman and then their shortstop. Maglie got the message.

There were several such serious confrontations. The press noticed the change, and some reporters started to criticize Jackie as a troublemaker. They criticized him even more when his newfound outspokenness was no longer limited to baseball matters and personalities. He spoke out on civil rights and voiced his opinions about nonbaseball issues. This, added to his short temper on the ball field, irritated both black and white baseball people.

They wanted him to keep in mind his special role as a pioneer before he shot off his mouth. Jackie believed, on the contrary, that being a pioneer imposed on him a duty to speak out on issues affecting other blacks. Outstanding black athletes like Joe Louis before him, or Roy Campanella after him, minded their own business. Jackie felt, though, that baseball was part of a larger, serious world and that he could not just mind his own business. Larry Doby had it right when he said that Jackie "[is] about the only one of us who is in a position to say exactly what's on his mind," and Jackie took advantage of that situation.

When the other blacks in baseball were asked about charges of white racism and answered evasively, Jackie refrained from criticizing them for not backing him. He saw it rather as another case of the media pitting those blacks who were timid and afraid of losing what they had against those, like himself, who would settle for nothing less than justice for all their people.

Jackie became a spokesman not just for blacks but for all players as well. He was a trailblazer for the future players' union. Once, when he was fined by the league president, he refused to pay until he was granted a hearing, an unheard-of demand.

As a result, Jackie received much new publicity in 1949. Other Dodgers might complain in the clubhouse about something, but Jackie was the only one willing to be quoted. He always made good press. He spoke his mind; he did it clearly; he stood by his words. He would end by telling reporters they could quote him. And when controversy over those words erupted, he would not claim that he had been misquoted.

As Doby implied, Jackie alone had the superstar visibility, the insight, the outrage, the articulateness, and the love of controversy that allowed him to be the lightning rod for other blacks and other players. Never at a loss for words, he was also quick to dash off a letter whenever he saw something he did not like. If he had to live life over again, he said late in life, he would do it the same way.

He became controversial now not because he was black but because he appeared hotheaded and outspoken. He saw his critics as racist, and they saw him as self-centered. Jackie had gotten past the obvious racism that prevented blacks from enjoying success. For the first time he ran into a special racism known to those blacks who have "made it." A lot of people had rooted for him as long as he was the underdog. They liked the silent, cheek-turning black who appealed to the white man's sense of decency and who gratefully received any favors the white man chose to give. According to this subtle form of racism, a black man is acceptable in the ballpark at the price of not having an equal opportunity to let off steam.

Jackie's accomplishments in baseball were to white Americans proof that the American dream worked. It blinded them to the fact that it had worked only belatedly and reluctantly for an outstanding black man and not at all for the average black. Many moderate white Americans thought that the important things were to integrate baseball and stop lynchings in the South. After that, there were no big obstacles left, and if African Americans did not enter the mainstream of society, it was their own fault. These people did not understand that second-class citizenship for blacks was so old and widespread in every area of American life that it had to be fought against inch by inch. As Jackie said, "The fight has just begun."

On the other hand, he had a certain intolerance himself. He would not allow people to legitimately disagree with him. He overworked the words *bigot* and *racist*. People had to point out to him that while much of the jockeying and many of the brushback pitches were due to hatred of blacks, they also were due to something that had little to do with his skin—his competitiveness and his greatness, his intensity, his daring, his superior skill, his rattling of opponents on the bases, and his stealing bases even when it was not necessary to win a game. Also some of it was due to jealousy of the man who beat them in so many different ways. Any successful batter has to expect pitchers and benches to make him uncomfortable at the plate. But with his long history of fighting racism wherever he ran across it, Jackie had difficulty understanding this viewpoint.

Jackie began to see most of the press corps as his enemies. He ignored the fact that they wrote for the reader who turned to the sports pages to read about baseball, not about the state of the world. The reporters seemed to him untruthful and ready to blow things out of proportion. Sometimes even black reporters had to defend the press against his charges.

More and more Jackie would be friendly only with those journalists who saw things his way and cold to those who did not. He got into squabbles with the influential baseball columnist Dick Young. Young had defended Jackie in the early days but had been turned off by Jackie's growing interest in racial politics. Believing that ballplayers should stick to what they do best, Young accused Jackie of getting a swelled head. Jackie in turn accused Young of being bigoted.

Maybe both were right. Not every player has to stick to just playing baseball. And maybe Jackie, besides being a black activist, did have a swelled head. Jackie's speaking out for the rights of fellow blacks and fellow players did not rule out the possibility that he might love to hear his own voice and views.

Jackie often got into trouble because he was right when other people were wrong. In Cincinnati, the black ballplayers were allowed into the hotel with the team on condition that they ate in their rooms. One day, when a series of events made it difficult to get a meal that way, Jackie decided to defy this arrangement. Bracing himself for the worst, he went with his wife to the hotel dining room. The host led them to a table and left. He reappeared with a baseball and a pen, asking for an autograph. "I've been waiting all season for you to come in here, Jackie," he said excitedly.

This incident proved that many of the fears about breaking the color line were the delusions of cowards. It proved Jackie's and Rickey's point that segregation was not set in stone, but would often crumble if those opposing it took the trouble to challenge it peacefully.

* * *

Rickey's prediction that the unshackling of Jackie would help his performance proved correct. If 1947 was Jackie's most heroic year, 1949 was his greatest year statistically. Unlike in 1948, his weight and conditioning were perfect. Things seemed to be going his way from the very start of the year, even in the Deep South.

After the successful tour of some Southern states in the spring of the previous year, Rickey added Florida and Georgia to the 1949 tour. Local officials and fans were delighted to see Jackie in action. The feeling was not mutual. Georgia was his native state, and Jackie hated even being there. When he came to bat for the first time, he felt paralyzed. He had good reason. The Ku Klux Klan had threatened his life.

When warned by the Klan not to play in Atlanta, Rickey changed his strategy. In the past he would cancel games. Now he felt that baseball had come a long way. He would no longer avoid confrontation. Told that Jackie might be mobbed, he replied, "Yes, by autograph seekers!" The Dodgers played the Atlanta Crackers on April 8 through 10. The crowds, half of them black, broke all attendance records. There was no incident. The only assault on Jackie was, as Rickey had predicted, by autograph hounds and fans. For good measure he batted .412 in the four games there.

The Dodgers played in other Southern cities—in South Carolina, Texas, Georgia, and Florida—without incident and with large crowds. The federal government's desegregating the armed forces in July 1948 had proved that baseball and Jackie Robinson were in the forefront of peaceful social change.

At the end of the first half of the regular 1949 season, Jackie led the league in almost all important hitting categories. He came in first in the fans' voting for the National League All-Star team.

14

THE SPOKESMAN
(1949-1950)

In July 1949 Jackie began a new career as a spokesman for black people, not just black players. It would be a long and sometimes stormy one. Some would say that when he left the field of athletic competition, Jackie got into matters that were over his head; others that his vision expanded as he matured. He went from addressing soluble problems in the little corner of America called baseball to heroically tackling more complex problems in the society at large, problems that still have not been solved.

The years right after World War II had seen the beginning of the cold war between democratic, capitalist America (and Western Europe) and authoritarian, communist Soviet Russia (and Eastern Europe). Americans worried that Russia might try to conquer Western Europe, or even the world. A number of Americans had become Communists as a way out of the Great Depression in the 1930s. Now there was a worry that they would be loyal to Communist Russia.

There was widespread fear of Communist expansion overseas and Communist spying and treason at home. The tensions of the cold war created an atmosphere of hysteria and witch-hunts, as congressmen and self-appointed patriots started looking for Communists everywhere. A ready target was Paul Robeson.

An all-star black athlete at Rutgers University, Robeson had had a varied career as lawyer, singer, and actor. He was an immensely talented man whose career had often run into the hurdles created by racism and segregation. Like Jackie, he was one to speak out. He had now grown so embittered by life in America that he had become a Communist. He spoke lovingly of Russia as a place free of racism. He particularly enraged white America by declaring that "American Negroes would not fight in case of a war against Russia."

One of the prominent Communist-hunting groups was the House Un-American Activities Committee. It now invited Jackie to come down and testify in opposition to Robeson. In a way, this was quite a compliment. The committee was pushing Jackie into a role he was just beginning to take for himself: spokesman for African Americans and their problems. By sheer coincidence, the committee's invitation came at the very time that the new outspoken Jackie was surfacing.

Still, the invitation put Jackie in perhaps the worst dilemma in his life. He had become caught up in the domestic cold war—in the cross fire between American Communists and Communist-haters. He had greatly admired Robeson as a man and as a spokesman for blacks. Now he was being asked to defend his own Americanism by attacking a fellow black man, and a great one at that.

Robeson, ironically, had been the one who had in 1943 asked Commissioner Landis to let blacks into organized baseball and who had in 1945 actually picketed the New York Yankee offices. By such pressures, he helped prepare the way for Jackie. On the other hand, while Robeson had a right to his views, he had no right to claim to speak for all African Americans on the matter of choosing between America and Russia.

For a black man, as Jackie had discovered in the army, there were two wars: one against foreign enemies and another against the racists at home. Jackie saw Robeson's remark as useful in the home-front war because it could frighten white America into dealing decently with blacks. But it also could frighten white America into believing that blacks were disloyal revolutionaries and should be oppressed even more.

The irony was that a congressman from Georgia was asking Jackie—whose family had fled the state and who still could not get a cup of coffee in a decent dining place of his choosing there—to defend the American way of life. Most whites obviously had no idea of how blacks lived and the depth of the frustration that caused Robeson's bitter remark. To attack Robeson would be to attack all blacks who were trying to enlighten those whites and who had the guts to speak out against the racism and the hypocrisy of white America.

Jackie was bombarded with letters and phone calls

from all sorts of individuals and groups urging him to take this or that stand. He spent long hours with Rachel and with others discussing the matter. He believed that he was not yet knowledgeable and experienced enough to be a national voice for African Americans in the political arena. Still, Rickey thought it important for baseball and for blacks that Jackie answer Robeson.

On July 18 Jackie appeared before the committee. He gave a prepared speech. He had received help in drafting it from Rickey and from some black intellectuals, but most of it was in his own words. He began by saying that he was an expert not on communism or any other kind of political "ism" but "on being a colored American, with thirty years of experience at it." In a difficult balancing act, he proceeded in effect to say, "a plague on both your houses."

Robeson's words he called "very silly." Whites had, nevertheless, a lot of homework to do to make sure there was real democracy in America. If blacks hated communism for not being democratic, they would also hate the nondemocratic aspects of America —the discrimination in the army and on the job, the segregation in public facilities. These evils existed and had to be gotten rid of even if some of the people decrying them were Communists. Jackie's main point was that complaints about racial injustice were not fabricated by Communists, but were well known to all African Americans and were merely being exploited by the Communists. Get rid of communism and you would still have injustice in America.

Jackie's testimony received wide publicity. One headline said, JACKIE HITS A DOUBLE—AGAINST COMMUNISTS AND JIM CROW [segregation]. Most whites, conveniently focusing on the attack on Robeson and ignoring the attack on injustice in America, overwhelmingly approved it. Some liberals and some blacks thought that Jackie had sold out. A few weeks later, people attending a Paul Robeson concert had stones thrown at them at the very time that Jackie was being given an award by conservative whites for his remarks to the committee. This took place in the democratic America he had just, in part, defended. Jackie himself would in his last years come to regret his testimony.

Right after testifying, Jackie put on his uniform and played in a night game, where he put on one of his splendid performances in an area where he *was* an expert.

During this season the last traces of racism on the Dodgers team seemed to disappear as the talented trio of black players, Campanella, Newcombe, and Robinson, put on quite a show. The team had a terrific season. The arrival of Newcombe particularly helped Jackie. He had come up as part of Rickey's escalator strategy: First introduce Jackie in 1947, then Campanella in 1948, and now Newcombe in 1949. A tall, hard-throwing pitcher, Newcombe provided some additional protection at the plate for Jackie and Campanella. Opposing teams knew that if they threw beanballs at the two black sluggers, they would get them from Newcombe in turn. There is nothing like the fear of retaliation to civilize some people.

Jackie ended the year batting a league-leading and major league career high of .342. He played in all 154 games, a remarkable feat considering all the spikings and attempted beanings. He was fifth in the league in total bases; fourth in doubles (38); third in slugging percentage (.528), runs scored (122), and triples (12); and second in RBIs (124) and hits (203). He also hit 16 home runs and stole a league-leading 37 bases. He was first among second basemen participating in double plays.

Two years after being named Rookie of the Year, he received the coveted Most Valuable Player of the Year award. He was no longer a social trailblazer, just a very great baseball player. One sportswriter said that he was the best second baseman in the National League and the most dangerous player in all of baseball. He was more dangerous than Stan Musial or Ted Williams because he combined power with speed and with fielding. Again comparisons were being made with Cobb for his skill in upsetting not just pitchers but entire teams.

With his leadership and his eagerness for victory, he kept on inspiring the Dodgers. He knew, for example, how to handle Don Newcombe. When victory in a game seemed certain, Newcombe tended to relax on the mound. Jackie would go over and call him terrible names. That made Newcombe so mad he took it out on the hitters and struck them out.

The Dodgers won their second pennant in three years, scoring 113 more runs than the second-place Cardinals and setting a new Dodger record for home runs. Almost every player had a career year. Some experts believe that the 1949 Dodgers were the greatest in Brooklyn history and that Jackie was a vital part of one of the great infields in baseball history.

Again, as in 1947, they faced the New York Yankees. Unfortunately, the World Series was an anticlimax for both the Dodgers and for Jackie. He batted an anemic .188, and they lost the series in a mere five games.

Jackie's salary needed some attending to. In his rookie year he made the standard minimum of $5,000. When it came time, after the splendid achievement of 1947, to discuss 1948, he was offered the same salary. He was stunned. He and Rachel, not used to business ways, had to be told that that was only an initial offering, part of the ritual of negotiations. He finally received $12,500. In 1949 his salary went up to $20,000. Stan Musial made $80,000 that year. Because of his sense of mission and his gratitude to the Dodgers, Jackie did not become a holdout.

Now in late 1949, Jackie asked for his salary to be raised from $20,000 to $50,000. That was quite an increase, but it was equal to his achievement. He had made the racial breakthrough. He had played a key role in the Dodgers winning two pennants. He had been Rookie of the Year and then Most Valuable Player. He had won the league batting championship. He had been a terrific fielder and base stealer. Above all, he had done wonders for attendance, even in exhibition games, even in the South. He had put many hundreds of thousands, probably millions, of dollars into the pockets of the Dodgers' owners.

For all of his noble role in the Jackie Robinson story, however, Rickey was known among some journalists as "El Cheapo." He believed that keeping salaries low made players hungry and eager to win. He could be angered even over a request for a $5,000 increase. So Jackie had to settle for a $35,000 salary for 1950. It was the highest salary ever for a Dodger, but that same year Yankee Joe DiMaggio was getting $100,000.

Fortunately Jackie had other sources of income. The idea of making a movie out of his life story had come up in late 1947. The script made the rounds of the studios without gaining acceptance because the concept of a black man as the hero of a movie was ahead of its time. Hollywood was not ready to follow baseball into new territory.

Finally in early 1950 the movie, *The Jackie Robinson Story*, went into production. Soon after the birth of daughter Sharon in January, Robinson went to Hollywood to star in it. It was filmed in three weeks. Making the Hollywood scene was a new adventure for him. He had certainly taken a giant step from the poverty-stricken black section of Pasadena to the nearby glittering world of the movie colony.

To cover those few miles had taken many years, much frustration and uncertainty, and plenty of hard work. Jackie now had an experience that few people in history have had: playing himself in a movie about his own heroic life. He received $50,000 for his acting and a share of the profits from the movie. As for the movie itself, Jackie came to realize later that it was done too early, too quickly, and too cheaply to be as good as it could have been. Around the time that the movie opened later that year, Jackie appeared on the cover of *Life*, in those days the biggest mass-circulation magazine in the country.

As the family was growing and as the income from baseball playing and from the increasing number of side activities grew, Jackie and Rachel were able, in July 1948, to move from the working-class black neighborhood of Bedford-Stuyvesant into a comfortable duplex apartment in the middle-class white neighborhood of Flatbush, near Ebbets Field. Jackie hoped it would not be Pasadena all over again. One day, when Jackie and Rachel looked for Jack, Jr., who had wandered off, they found him at a neighbor's home having a cookie. The combination of the boy's cuteness and the father's fame helped create good neighbors.

Soon the Robinsons were ready to buy their own home. They found a nice house in the St. Albans section of the borough of Queens. The Campanellas lived there, as well as such famous black performers as the jazz bandleader Count Basie.

15

JACKIE'S WAY
(1950-1951)

In many ways, 1947 and 1949 were Jackie's greatest years. After that, clouds began to gather. He was 30 now, an age when most baseball players begin their decline. In 1950 Jackie batted .328, an excellent average but a falloff from the preceding year. The Dodgers, with perhaps the best team in the league, lost the pennant in storybook fashion in the bottom of the ninth inning of the last game of the season on a simple misjudgment in baserunning.

A major setback to Jackie was the sudden departure in late 1950 of his mentor, Branch Rickey. One of the co-owners of the team, Walter O'Malley, was able through legal maneuvers to force Rickey out. The change was not good news for Jackie. Except for the money question, the Robinson-Rickey relationship was one of the great ones in sports history. It cut across age, race, class, and temperament. The two men understood and respected each other. Rickey was always on call when needed, inspiring and encouraging Jackie, protecting him, giving advice, looking after his interests. He was a sort of father to Jackie, who never had a father. And Rickey admitted that he learned a lot in return.

The new man in charge, O'Malley, was a corporate attorney who cared only for the public image. He disliked Rickey's style and all people brought in or favored by Rickey. As a result, Jackie knew that things would become more difficult for him.

Another of Jackie's guiding lights, manager Burt Shotton, was ousted by O'Malley. He was replaced by Chuck Dressen, who had been a coach under Durocher. Yet a third ouster was that of Commissioner Chandler. The owners were unhappy with the commissioner in part because he had ignored them when they had been against bringing blacks into major league baseball.

So in a matter of weeks, the three men who had most to do with Jackie's entry into baseball were gone. Jackie would be on his own. Now, of course, he was important and independent enough to be able to handle himself. But he missed the presence of Rickey the friend.

For Jackie, 1951 was another great year. He batted .338 and hit nineteen home runs. His fielding percentage of .992 set a new major league record for second basemen. Having participated in a record-setting 133 double plays in the previous year, he improved on that number this year with 137. For the Dodgers, however, the 1951 season was a painful one. They jumped to an early lead while the Giants, still managed by Durocher, lost eleven straight games. On August 11 the Dodgers led the Giants by thirteen and a half games.

There followed one of the greatest pennant races in history. The Dodgers stopped hitting and managed to win only half their games. The Giants put together a series of great winning streaks, including one of sixteen games, and threatened to catch up. In the end, for the third year in a row, a whole season's work came down to the last game of the season. The Dodgers were playing the Phillies, and in that game, Jackie put on what many regard as his greatest performance. In the bottom of the twelfth inning of a tied game, the Phillies had the bases loaded and two out. The batter hit a line drive. Jackie made an unbelievable dive, caught the ball, and almost knocked himself out rolling over on the ground. He was carried back to the dugout and lay on the bench, unable to go out to the field in the next inning. Reese, the team leader, insisted that he continue playing, because he was so badly needed. The Giants had won their game that day and now led by a half game. The Dodgers had to win. Jackie forced himself up and resumed play. In the top of the fourteenth inning he hit a home run to win the game. That was the kind of clutch playing that had made Jackie legendary.

For only the second time in National League history, the pennant race ended in a tie. The Dodgers and the Giants had to play a three-game play-off series. The teams split the first two games. In the third game, one of the most famous in baseball history, the Dodgers were leading 4–1. Newcombe indicated in the seventh inning that he was tired. Jackie, as usual, berated him and insisted that he keep on pitching. And, as usual, Newcombe responded by striking out the other side in the eighth inning. In the ninth, though, trouble developed. Newcombe had to be relieved. Ralph Branca then gave up the "shot heard round the world," the three-run homer by Bobby Thomson that won the game, 5–4. The Dodgers had performed the unheard-of feat of losing the pennant in the bottom of the ninth inning of the last game for two years in a row.

One of the first Dodgers to congratulate Durocher and the Giants in their clubhouse was Jackie. He said to them, "We didn't lose it; you guys won it." His old enemy Leo Durocher thought that that showed real class. But Durocher was not the only one to appreciate Jackie. One poll of American boys revealed that Jackie ranked with Joe DiMaggio as favorite athletes.

The Most Valuable Player award went to Roy Campanella. He richly deserved it, as Jackie himself admitted. Yet Jackie also suspected that racism was at work in a subtle way, because his own statistics were better than Campanella's. The journalists who did the voting had become irritated with the new, argumentative Jackie. He had seemed to them to allow celebrity status to go to his head. So they voted, Jackie believed, for Campanella, who was a "good" black, knowing his place and minding his own business.

As Jackie saw it, in the old days racism took the form of excluding blacks, period. Now that blacks were allowed in, a screening process took place. Excluded were those who talked too much about their rights instead of being grateful for the progress the whites allowed them to make. By voting for Campanella, the journalists had covered themselves against any charge of being antiblack at the very time that they were penalizing Jackie for being self-assertive.

This hidden racism would pit the traditional passive blacks against the new activist blacks, and Jackie's outspokenness caused some tension between him and Campanella. When racists bombed some African American houses of worship in the South, Jackie issued a strong condemnation, while Campanella merely said that blacks should stop pressing "to get too far too fast." Jackie was saddened by these words, which blamed the victim and gave the moral victory to the bigots.

When the Dodgers went to St. Louis, Jackie wanted for once to stay with the team at the Chase Hotel. Management was willing to put the blacks up only if they remained out of the dining room, lobby, and swimming pool. Campanella, not liking these conditions, wanted to continue staying in the black part of town. Jackie, though, insisted that staying at the Chase, even under these humiliating conditions, was still a foot in the door. Blacks had to swallow personal pride. By making a stand at every chance, moving forward inch by inch, they would help future African Americans break segregation down altogether.

The split between them was the split in the black community between the moderates or compromisers and the activists or idealists. Campanella said, "I'm no crusader. I'm a baseball player." This deeply bothered Robinson, who saw himself as both baseball player *and* crusader (and, in later years, only as crusader) and who believed that no African American could separate the two categories.

Campanella liked to say that Jackie owed everything to baseball. Jackie, on the other hand, believed that baseball merely gave him a chance which he richly deserved to exhibit his talent. He did as much for baseball as it did for him. Certainly the balance was uneven in money. Though the biggest draw in the game, he fell far short of being paid the kind of salary the top white players received.

Campanella did not like controversy. When black players had a complaint, Jackie acted as he had when he was a morale officer in the army faced with the plight of the black soldiers. He tried to get something changed. Campanella, on the other hand, told the complaining blacks that they should be happy about being big leaguers. Baseball had been good to them, and they should not aggravate things by being pushy.

Sports columnist Dick Young complained that with Campanella he could discuss baseball but with Jackie the discussion quickly turned to race relations and social issues, not topics of interest to sportswriters or their readers. No wonder that Campanella was liked by the reporters and Jackie was not. Jackie's reply was that he sought respect, not love.

Young said to Jackie: "When I talk to Campy, I almost never think of him as a Negro. Any time I talk to you, I'm acutely aware of the fact that you're a Negro."

Jackie answered that Campanella surely was a Negro when he tried to get into the Chase Hotel or buy a house. According to Jackie, Young really meant "a certain kind of Negro," the kind whites had for too long been used to.

The difference between them was not only philosophical but also temperamental. Campanella was laidback and likable; Jackie was intense, irritable, and irritating. Campanella could be teased, Jackie could not. Clubhouse horseplay was not for him. Every game was a championship contest he had to be ready for. It was typical of Jackie that when Bobby Thomson hit the game-winning home run in the 1951 play-offs and players and fans alike dissolved in the joy of victory or the dejection of sudden defeat, Jackie alone kept a cool head. He carefully watched to make sure that Thomson touched each base, as if playing by the book and making some technical point could still retrieve the game amid the pandemonium.

With the intensity that helped make Jackie great went a certain grating solemnity. Outstanding individuals—reformers, leaders, prophets—can be difficult to live with. They often lack a sense of humor, especially about themselves.

The good side of Jackie's heroism was his integrity. His strong sense of mission made him unwilling to remain merely a great ballplayer. He needed to use his prominence to help the less fortunate. He saw himself carrying forward what Robeson and Louis had begun. He was a man with an honorable mission. "Stay in school," he would say to adoring black youngsters wherever he went. As one who avoided alcohol and womanizing, he scolded other players for their excesses.

The bad side of his heroism, however, often cropped up. At various times, little things like being innocently offered some watermelon or hearing "Dixie" played at a Pee Wee Reese birthday party made him tense and critical. And not just with whites. He once chided Campanella and Newcombe for giving some kids chewing tobacco, saying, "It will rot their teeth."

Holding himself to the highest standards, he insisted that others do so too. When he saw black baseball spectators cheering when they were allowed into previously restricted seats, he rebuked them. Blacks, he said, had a perfect right to these seats, and no favors were being done them. At another time, he saw a group of drunken black baseball fans in the stands, and he started to berate them for their behavior.

There was something of the stern, puritan father, the teacher, or the drill sergeant about him. It made him a leader of men and a pioneer. It also made him a huge pain in the neck. Fighting the good fight against racism all his life had left his nerves ragged. Keeping the faith exacted its price. By 1956 it was observed that he "played with hate, played mad."

Curiously, the more militant Jackie got on better with his white teammates than with his fellow blacks.

He talked, dined, and played cards with the whites. In later years, he seemed unfriendly to young black stars like Bill White or Frank Robinson. The easygoing Campanella tended to hang out with black grounds-keepers and kitchen help rather than with his white teammates. Jackie insisted on being accepted by white society as an equal and, through sheer resolve, he was. Was that only because he was busy integrating the team and American society? Or was he also eager to flee the subjugation of his people and to make it into the comfortable white middle class? Maybe he himself did not know.

Pee Wee Reese, the outstanding shortstop from segregated Kentucky, was Jackie's closest friend on the team. A player on the pennant-winning 1941 team, he was a natural leader of a team whose stars mostly came up in the later 1940s. When he first heard that a black man was coming to the Dodgers, he was edgy. Like most Southerners, he believed that African Americans were not good enough to be in the majors. But he was open-minded. He would not have anything to do with the Walker petition. He took the lead to make Jackie feel at home. Once, on a golf course, when some Dodgers were playing in one group and Jackie was with another black man, Reese invited the blacks to join the group. He also invited Jackie to join the others at meals or card games or in bull sessions.

Perhaps the greatest moment came in Cincinnati in 1947, when the crowd, with many in it from nearby Kentucky, was yelling insults at Jackie. Reese walked over to confer with Jackie and, as he did so, put his arm around Jackie's shoulders. That hushed the spectators and sent an important signal to the baseball world.

Reese showed great understanding and sympathy. He said, "Frankly I don't think I'd stand up under the kind of thing he's been subjected to as well as he has."

It was not long before the two men were unofficial cocaptains, Reese the soft-spoken, easygoing white Southerner, and Robinson the hard-driving, dazzling black. On the baseball diamond they made a great fielding combination around second base, initiating a record-setting number of double plays. They were at the top of the batting order, adept at getting on base in many ways and then expert in working together on the double steal or the hit-and-run play (running before the batter makes contact with the ball). Together they were the very symbol of integration. In its quiet, private way, the friendship of Jackie and Pee Wee was a greater breakthrough for America than Jackie stealing bases to the thunderous roar of thousands.

16

THE GATHERING STORM
(1952-1956)

In 1952 Jackie's batting average went down to .308 (still a very good figure), but he tied his career high of nineteen home runs in one year. The entire Dodger lineup was very powerful in offense. For more than half a season the Dodgers won-lost record was at an almost incredible .750. They established a large lead over the rest of the league.

Then slowly it began to shrink. There were fears of a repeat of the 1951 disaster. But the Dodgers managed to straighten themselves out this time and finish far ahead of every other team. Again they met those awesome Yankees in another all New York "subway series," but they could not prevent a repetition of earlier disasters. Once again Brooklyn cried, "Wait till next year!"

The integration of baseball, now in its sixth year, was far from complete. Jackie was still being hit by pitched balls at a rate higher than average—twelve times in 1952. At one point in Cincinnati, he had to have armed guards outside the stadium because of a death threat. Yet Jackie was able to keep his cool through it all. When a reporter said to him, "This must be hell," Jackie snapped back, "Never been there." And there was the other "cool" way of handling the bigotry: In one game in which he played under a death threat, he got three hits, including a three-run homer.

In St. Louis, the Cardinals were calling him names again. Jackie was furious. He told a reporter, "I don't think I have to put up with it anymore." It was sad to realize that 1947 had not settled such things for good. The Cardinals manager was none other than Eddie Stanky, the Alabaman, who had been traded from the Dodger team. When the reporter asked Stanky what was going on, Stanky at first denied the whole thing. Then he said that it was "just routine bench jockeying" and not out of line.

When the baseball season was over and he might be expected to give the headline writers a rest, Jackie managed to remain embroiled in controversy over race. He appeared in November 1952 on the TV show "Youth Wants to Know." A teenager asked him if the Yankees were prejudiced against blacks. Jackie answered, "I think the Yankee management is prejudiced. There isn't a single Negro on the team now and very few in the entire Yankee farm system."

This remark caused one of the biggest disputes of his career. The evidence suggests that Jackie was merely telling the truth. It was an open secret that the Yankee management was afraid that African Americans on the team would attract black and Puerto Rican fans and drive away the middle-class suburbanites. Yet the Yankee officials vehemently denied the charge and Jackie was called a "rabble-rouser" and flooded with hate mail. Reprimanded for the remark by Commissioner Ford Frick, Jackie stuck to his guns. Frick told Jackie to feel free to speak out but to be sure he was on solid ground in making charges. Jackie took that to be support from someone in a position of power.

In the spring of 1953 Jackie found himself at the center of a new controversy involving race. Manager Dressen announced that a black rookie, Junior Gilliam, would play second base and Jackie would move over to third. Third baseman Billy Cox would be benched. Cox and several others complained about this rearrangement. Then, in a bar when he was drunk, Cox said to a reporter, "How would you like a nigger to take your job?"

Other players also commented on the racial overtones of the move. One Dodger then said something that is often heard in the upheaval of breaking the color line: "I don't mind them in the game, but now they're really taking over." That remark implied that, though the game was integrated, skin color rather than talent was still uppermost in white minds.

Some reporters were shocked that this could be happening on the team of the great Jackie Robinson experiment. Eventually, things got straightened out. There were apologies and reconciliations. Jackie, who at one point threatened to sue one of the newspapers over a version of this story, said that the Dodgers were still a model of racial harmony. According to a player, the source of the problem was not race but Jackie himself, who did not want to play third base.

Like it or not, during the 1953 season Jackie played both at third and at yet another new position for him, left field. The 1953 Dodgers were one of the greatest of all baseball teams. They probably had the finest lineup in National League history. At every position an all-star player performed. The team batted .285 and hit 208 home runs. It also made the fewest errors in the league, 118. Jackie, now thirty-four, batted .329, scored more than one hundred runs, and batted in more than ninety.

The Dodgers clinched the pennant on September 13, the earliest date in league history. They won 105 games and ended with a lead of 13 games. On paper, they should have smashed the Yankees, their perennial rival in the World Series. But the Dodgers had been beaten in all four World Series in which they had met the Yanks during the past dozen years. As if the Dodgers were jinxed, it happened again. Jackie did his best, batting .320 in the series. Though he was losing his speed, he turned in a good job in left field.

When in 1950 Rickey, Shotton, and Chandler left their jobs at the same time, Jackie was not left adrift after all. The new Brooklyn manager, Chuck Dressen, turned out to be Jackie's favorite of the four he would work under. Dressen, in turn, thought that Jackie was simply the best baseball player around. They got along excellently. When, as a result of a contract squabble, Dressen was let go in late 1953, Jackie and Pee Wee

Reese were the only Dodgers who called Dressen and urged him to stay.

O'Malley brought up Walt Alston, a man with no major league experience but with loyalty to O'Malley. As a rookie manager taking over a team of veterans and future Hall of Famers who had made it to first or second place year after year, he had a hard time earning their respect. Alston's biggest problem was Jackie. The two men could not get along. Jackie was a born leader, and now it was often remarked that, if he had been white, he would have become a manager. Alston saw Jackie as a rival, while Jackie saw Alston as a dummy. And Jackie was never one to hide his feelings. He acted as if Alston had stolen a job that really belonged to Dressen.

The tension between them grew during the 1954 season. Alston thought that an aging Jackie should become a utility player. He tried out another player at third base. Jackie, though, believed that he still had good years in him. As a matter of fact, in that season Jackie batted .311 and hit fifteen home runs, while Alston's new third baseman batted .245 and hit seven home runs. But between his own age and the manager's tinkering, Jackie for the first time did not play regularly at any one position. He played in 124 games (with fewer than 400 at bats), half of them in left field and half in the infield. Most telling was that he stole only seven bases. Clearly this was not the Jackie Robinson of old.

Their mutual dislike came to a head once when an

umpire made a questionable call. Jackie, as was his style these days, rushed out of the dugout to protest loudly. Alston, coaching at third base, did not move at all. The other Dodgers took their cue from the manager and sat still. Alston was annoyed over Jackie's independent action. Jackie in turn let it be known that, with a "wooden Indian" as a manager, the team would go nowhere. Word of Jackie's remark came to Alston.

Jackie liked managers to be aggressive, like Durocher and Dressen, rather than quiet, like Shotton and Alston. In this case, though, he had a good reason to be angry. Photos in the next day's newspaper showed that Jackie's complaint over the umpire's call was definitely correct.

With the team also doing poorly that year, Jackie for the first time talked about leaving baseball. Such thoughts may have been encouraged by the fact that Jackie's relations with the new owner, O'Malley, were as bad as those with Alston.

Jackie made no secret of his love for and admiration of Rickey. O'Malley thought of Jackie as an exhibitionist, a publicity hound, and a loudmouth. Jackie thought that O'Malley did not really believe in integration. When racists had bombed churches in the South and Jackie had condemned them, O'Malley had labeled Jackie's remarks "ill timed and intemperate." At another point, Jackie made his usual fuss about segregated quarters for the players in Miami during spring training. O'Malley asked him why, if the segregation there was acceptable to Jackie in 1947, it was not all right a few years later. Such a question revealed his

144

insensitivity to racism, to current events, and to the changing baseball scene.

Nor did O'Malley like Jackie as a person. Once, when Jackie chose not to play in some exhibition games in the spring because of an injury, O'Malley accused him of being lazy and called him a "prima donna" and a crybaby. At another time, when the Dodger bench rode an umpire over his call, the league president fined Jackie seventy-five dollars. Jackie had no objection to the fine but had strong objections to being singled out when others were involved too. He took the unprecedented step of protesting the president's action. To his dismay, he found that O'Malley was unwilling to back his own player.

Jackie's adversary in the newspaper world, Dick Young, wrote a story saying that some of the younger Dodgers resented Jackie's aggressive manner in protesting plays and his acting as if he were manager. In his reaction to the story, O'Malley seemed once again to be siding with others—with the players, with Young— against Jackie. Jackie was developing conflicts with the Dodgers front office at the same time that he became more outspoken in the clubhouse with teammates, on the field with umpires and opponents, and off the field with reporters.

When a third child, David, was born in 1952, the house in St. Albans had become too small. Also, the local school, after integration, was becoming all black. This was no more satisfactory to Jackie than an all-white school would have been. Jackie now had the

145

financial capacity to have a house built to his specifica-
tions, and during 1952–1953 he and Rachel devoted a
lot of time to looking for the right location. He wanted
a place with an integrated school system near a body
of water for swimming and boating.

They ran into the quiet discrimination that affects
middle-class blacks who want to move into affluent
areas. Properties that were listed for sale had, suspi-
ciously, been sold just minutes before when the owner
or real estate agent discovered that the cultivated voice
on the phone belonged to a black man. In New York
and Connecticut, where they were looking, no one ever
said that blacks were not wanted. Properties just had
a way of suddenly disappearing from the market. Being
the great Jackie Robinson did not help. He ran into
the paradox that was common with integration. People
were willing to root for him at the ballpark but did not
want him living next door.

A reporter was alerted to Jackie's problem and
wrote an article on the discrimination he had run into.
A group of liberal-minded people in Stamford, Connecticut, made a commitment to help Jackie and Rachel find a place. Finally in 1954 they were able to
puchase a five-acre lot in that town. Jackie and Rachel
had a house built, and in 1955 the family moved in.
He and Rachel became part of the community. Their
children did all the middle-class, suburban things: the
Cub Scouts, the Brownies, the Little League, ballet
classes. Still, the nearby country club would not accept
Jackie Robinson as a member.

The 1954 season had been a bad year for Jackie

in many ways, not only because the team performed poorly. He was at odds with the head of the Dodgers organization, Walter O'Malley. He could not respect the manager, Walt Alston. He was having feuds with many of the reporters. He had become unpopular with umpires, with opponents, with teammates, and even, as in the case of Campanella, with fellow black players. He acted as though every strike called on him by the umpire was the result of bigotry. He was growing tired of all these wars.

The veterans of the great Dodgers team were aging, and some had been traded. The new younger players seemed to resent his aggressiveness. Most importantly, he also was aging. He was thirty-six. His hair was becoming white. His speed had diminished. He no longer had his own position on the field. He no longer could count on playing every day. And though he was still a .300 hitter, some of his other statistics had started to sink.

Perhaps it really was time to get out of baseball. He went so far as to write part of an article for *Look*, a high-circulation magazine, which had paid him handsomely for the right to be the first to reveal his retirement. When push came to shove, however, he could not get himself to do it. He felt he still had some baseball life in him. He was not a quitter. He tore up the article. He put on his glove and got ready to fight hard for that third base job.

He would have to compete as intensely as he had when breaking in nearly a decade earlier. An aging athlete is like a rookie in this regard. Alston again wanted Jackie in a utility role. But Alston was in a dilemma. If he stood up to Jackie, he would alienate the veterans; if he backed down, he would lose face with the younger players. Either way, he could lose his job.

During spring training in 1955, Alston would not say whether third base would go to Jackie or to the young prospect from the previous year. Jackie resorted to asking Dick Young what was up. He complained that playing one game out of four was no way to prepare himself for the season. He deserved to be in the lineup, he said, even if Alston did not understand that.

When Alston read these observations in Young's column, he exploded. At a team meeting, he complained about players who run to reporters with their problems. Then he added comments about someone having shot his mouth off about "who's a wooden Indian" and it had to stop. Jackie rose and answered sharply. There was a shouting match. The two men had to be prevented by other players from coming to blows.

Actually the whole team was dissatisfied over the way the veterans were being pushed into new field positions. Jackie was merely, as usual, the one with the guts to speak out.

In this battle of wills, Alston finally won. He established his credentials as boss. The results were that the team did very well; Jackie did very poorly. The 1955 Dodgers won their first 10 games, 22 of the first 24, and had an early 10-game lead. They won the National League pennant by 13½ games and clinched on the earliest date ever, September 6. They led the league in just about every statistic. Few teams in history could match that.

In the middle of all this wealth, Jackie was poverty-stricken. It was his worst year. Mainly platooning at third base, Jackie had injuries which made him miss a third of all the games. He found it difficult to keep his eye and rhythm while on the bench. He hit .256, his lowest ever, and had thirty-six RBIs. His fielding fell off too, as he made ten errors for an average of .966. Weighing thirty pounds more than in 1947 and 1949, he had slowed down. Tense relations with O'Malley and Alston did not help matters. The press saw him as a has-been. Perhaps it really was his last year.

In spite of all this misery, he was able to recoup some glory in the World Series. Though he batted only .182, his four hits and five runs scored came in clutch situations. In the first game he stole home. After the Dodgers lost the first two games and seemed still jinxed against those Yankees, Jackie led the team to a comeback at Ebbets Field. With the score tied at 2–2, Jackie singled. As he threatened to steal, he distracted the pitcher, who hit the batter. A perfect bunt loaded the bases and put Jackie on third. There his repeated threats to steal home so confused the pitcher that he walked the batter on four pitches and forced in a run. The famous antics of the "creaky old man," the "old gray fat man," as some called him, had driven another pitcher to the showers and sparked a Dodger resurgence.

A few innings later, Jackie doubled. As he rounded

second, he pretended to return to the base. The outfielder threw to second, whereupon Jackie raced to third. The hasty throw from second to third was high and late. He then scored on a single. As one writer put it, Jackie "had shown the world that the Dodgers can beat the Yankees." And that they did. For the first and only time, they won a World Series. The borough went insane with delight. This was the long awaited "next year."

Would there be a next year for Jackie? Though a nine-year veteran at the age of thirty-seven, he thought he had one more good year in him. He would recapture his triumphs and then retire in full glory. He said: "Baseball is just like a poker game. Nobody wants to quit when he's losing; nobody wants you to quit when you're ahead."

The 1956 season turned out, however, to be a hard one for him. Truth was he was not the only one aging. Many of the stars were. The Dodger dynasty seemed to be ending. The Milwaukee Braves led the league during most of the season. Still, Jackie was able to show his former skill—and help the team—in one of the great moments of his career, during a July series against the Braves.

Alston had tried others at third base, but with the team floundering, he brought Jackie back. In the first game of that series, Jackie's contributions were a clutch home run and a game-saving top-of-the-ninth double play. In the bottom of the same inning, Reese singled and was sacrificed to second. Carl Furillo was intentionally walked to get Jackie at the plate for a more likely out and to set up a possible double play. How the times had changed! On the third pitch, though, Jackie got a double for the victory. He was hitting and fielding again as in the old days.

With Jackie back in the lineup, the team came alive. They went on to beat the Braves in the remaining two games of the series. They overtook them in the pennant race and won the pennant by one game. The young Jackie resurfaced from time to time. In one game he walked and, teasing and taunting the pitcher for the Chicago Cubs, ran wild on the bases and scored the winning run. He still could practice the art of distraction, which he had perfected, under Rickey's tutelage, a decade before.

For the sixth time in nine years, the Dodgers were in the World Series. Jackie was tired, injured, patched up. He had a moment of glory in the sixth game, getting his last career hit. In the tenth inning of a scoreless game, with Gilliam on second, Duke Snider was walked in order to get at Jackie. He sent the ball into deep left field for a hit that drove in the winning run. His hit tied the series at three games each. That was the excitement and the heroics of the Jackie of old. In the seventh game, Jackie was, symbolically, the last batter. Also symbolically, he struck out.

That was the end of Jackie's baseball career.

That was the end of the Brooklyn dynasty.

17

LIFE AFTER BASEBALL
(1956)

With the end of another season, the question of retirement came up again. Jackie had told Rachel for several years that he would retire, but nothing had come of it. When he talked that way again now, she was a little skeptical.

He was approaching thirty-eight. He had lost his agility and grace. The bases were no longer easy to steal. His knees bothered him. His batting average in the last two years was seriously below .300 for the first time in his career. For the past three years he had felt unwanted by the Dodgers organization. The ever hostile O'Malley often talked of trading him. Baseball was no longer fun. It was time to move on to new challenges, more important matters.

It awaited only an opportunity to make up Jackie's mind. He realized that because he was black and because he had been controversial, he had no chance for a managerial or front-office job in baseball. For several years he had been looking for opportunities outside baseball. He refused to consider any position that made him a token black or a figurehead whose name was exploited. He wanted to have work to do, responsibility to bear, challenges to overcome.

Leaving baseball became inevitable when Chock Full o'Nuts made Jackie a nice offer. Chock was a successful fast-food chain in the New York area. Though owned by a white man, named Black, it was one of the first companies to go out of its way to hire minorities. Three-fourths of its employees were black.

On December 10, 1956, William Black met with Jackie and offered him the job of vice-president and director of personnel. His mission was to deal with excessive absenteeism and turnover of employees. He was to be a role model who would see that the workers were more satisfied on the job and the company more efficient. This was a great honor for Jackie. Baseball had brought a vice-presidency to a man who had never held a white-collar job and whose highest aspiration as a young man had been to be a school athletic coach.

Around the same time, Jackie was finally going to write an article about his retirement for *Look* magazine. He would get fifty thousand dollars for the surprise announcement, which would reach some forty million readers. He was sworn to secrecy so that the article would have maximum impact. He therefore never told the Dodger management of his plan.

A Dodger official telephoned Jackie on the day before the signing with Chock and the meeting with the editors of *Look*. He wanted to set up an important meeting. Jackie was evasive. He had to stall for a day.

He could not tell the official of his plan to leave baseball, because once the story was leaked, the *Look* article would lose its value as a scoop. Then, on December 12, right after signing the contracts with Chock and with *Look*, Jackie returned the call from the Dodgers. He was told that they had traded him to the New York Giants.

Jackie was stunned. He had always been a Dodger. Even before his baseball career, he had rooted for the Dodgers in the 1941 World Series. It was a blow to his never small ego to think that the Dodgers would actually trade him after all he had done for them, for baseball, for blacks, and for America. The only good thing in this development was the thought that he had beaten them to the punch. He had quit baseball before baseball got the chance to dump him.

Despite Jackie's request that they hold off, the Giants announced the trade on December 13. Jackie answered evasively the questions of the many reporters descending upon him. This meekness was highly unusual for him. The reason became clear a few days later, when *Look* came out with the article announcing his retirement from baseball. Just like almost a decade earlier, with the suspension of Durocher and the promotion of Jackie within twenty-four hours, the two news stories, back to back, were earthquakes in the world of sports.

As so often happened in Jackie's career, an explosion of controversy now occurred. He had, it was said, embarrassed and affronted the baseball owners by allowing the two teams to deal for him even though he knew he would never play again. And he had affronted the press corps assigned to him all those years by depriving them of a press conference for the full story of his retirement. Instead he had sold that hot sports story to a nonsports magazine for personal profit.

Many now jumped on him for being devious, money-grubbing, and selfish. This was how he rewarded baseball for all that it had done for him. The thin-skinned Jackie, of course, took this personally. He was tired of always being told he owed a lot to the game. He felt no guilt. His theory was that everyone resented the fact that he had outsmarted organized baseball.

Some reporters came to Jackie's defense, pointing out that he owed them nothing. On the contrary, by being outspoken, *he* had been the one player the press could always rely on to give them material for a good story or column. It can also be said in Jackie's defense that even if he did act selfishly and deviously in this matter, the lords of baseball—the owners and executives—always looked out for themselves first. A player should have the right to exercise the same sort of self-interest.

The Giants thought that his mind could be changed. They offered him $60,000 (he had been making $45,000) plus lavish retirement benefits. They were willing to go higher, even to have Jackie name his own sum. It was tempting. So was the outcry from the fans for his return. Jackie hesitated.

Then came a new blow. A Dodger official suggested

to the press that the *Look* article was just a ploy by Jackie to raise his salary by making himself hard to get. That did it for Jackie. He now had no choice but to leave for good if he wanted to keep his self-respect. If he stayed on, there would always be the suspicion that he had been devious in the way the official had suggested. He would be called a phony, and the great experiment that started out so nobly would end ignobly. That remark reminded Jackie that he had had enough of baseball and its shenanigans. To be accused of greed by the Dodger management was too much. So he who had started controversy as the first black in baseball now left as the most controversial black again.

Jackie regretted retiring, especially because it disappointed Jack, Jr. But the regret lasted only until the beginning of the next season. On opening day of 1957 his knees hurt so badly that he could hardly get out of bed. He knew then that he had done the right thing.

He left behind him a tremendous set of statistics. In ten years, he had a lifetime batting average of .311 and a total of 197 stolen bases. If there had been no segregation and he had played in the majors for another ten years, from ages 18 to 27, when players are at their peak physically, his lifetime records would have been even better.

As it was, he had been Rookie of the Year, Most Valuable Player, batting champion, fielding champion, stolen base champion, and double play champion (and record breaker). He led second basemen in double plays for four consecutive years. Six times he batted over .300 and scored over a hundred runs. Stealing home is a rare feat; many players never do it. Jackie did it no less than twenty times.

If in individual statistics he is bettered by others, as an overall player he was the greatest of his time. Certainly he was the most dangerous player, the greatest clutch performer, and the greatest competitor. And he was one of the most exciting and magnetic players in the history of the game.

Jackie's retirement marked the end of the great Dodger era that had begun with his arrival a decade earlier. From 1947 through 1956 the Dodgers were at the top of the National League. They ranked with the New York Giants of the early 1920s under John J. McGraw; and with the New York Yankees of Ruth and Gehrig in the later 1920s, of DiMaggio in the late 1930s and the 1940s, of Mantle and Berra in the 1950s. The Dodgers won six pennants in ten years, tying for first place in one of the nonchampionship years and missing first place on the last day of the season in another. In the other two years, they never finished below third place.

The victories meant fan enthusiasm. Before this time, the Dodgers had rarely drawn more than a million in attendance. In Jackie's ten years they drew over a million each year. In 1947 alone they drew 1.8 million.

Jackie had come up at the same time as most of the other all-star and Hall of Fame Dodgers. Together they had created a victorious baseball machine that was almost unique in remaining basically unchanged for a decade. His skills, zest, and leadership made him the outstanding player of that historic team.

Now they were aging, and Jackie's retirement signaled the beginning of the end of the great adventure. In late 1956 O'Malley began to dispose of Dodgers property. In 1957, the first year without Jackie, the Dodgers barely managed to stay out of the second half of the league. And at the end of that season the announcement was made that the Dodgers were moving to Los Angeles. Brooklyn went into shock and then mourning. A whole way of life was over.

Jackie's impact went far beyond the Dodgers. Once baseball desegregated, the other sports quickly followed: professional football in 1946, basketball in 1947, then golf and tennis. By the late 1950s blacks were on all major league baseball teams. As if having to catch up, they were winning awards and individual championships far out of proportion to the percentage of blacks in the population. Men like Maury Wills, Lou Brock, and Willie Mays followed Jackie in bringing back the daring running game that was typical early in the century. The next generation of black stars attacked the records established by Ruth, Cobb, and company. Truly Jackie had revolutionized the game and the society.

Jackie was, in fact, much more than a baseball star. He was a great black man and a great American who came to his greatness by way of sports, the way Frederick Douglass came to it by writing, George Washington Carver by science, Martin Luther King,

Jr., by his ministry, and Jesse Jackson by his oratory. Certainly Jackie now saw himself as much more than just an all-around athlete or a top baseball player. As soon as his playing days were over, he turned away from baseball to what he thought were more important things.

Now, he rarely watched baseball on TV. He never attended a Yankee game (the only team in town from 1958–1961) or a Mets game. The baseball that had made him great and famous seemed remote to him. After leaving it, he said that he did not miss it at all. When Ebbets Field was torn down, amid nostalgia and lamentations, to make room for apartment buildings, he said that the apartments were needed and were more important than monuments to mere baseball.

18

CRUSADER
(1956-1960)

Jackie now began a period of fifteen years which held mixed blessings. On the one hand, he had good jobs, fine salaries, respectable and honorific titles. He lived comfortably in a home in suburbia built to his taste. He had the proud awareness that he had by his own efforts fought his way out of poverty and oppression.

On the other hand, he seemed to twist and turn. The vice-presidency at Chock and the other enterprises he became involved in were not what playing second base before 35,000 worshipful fans had been. In politics, he wavered, to the annoyance of colleagues and followers. In civil rights he seemed to be radical and pushy to some and an Uncle Tom or "wannabe" to others.

In the days of integrating baseball, it was somehow easier, despite all the opposition and harassment, to know what to do and to go out with clenched teeth to do it. Now, with segregation officially dead, subtler forms of racism emerged that were harder to pinpoint and to overcome. In the divisions over the Vietnam War and the civil rights movement, it was difficult to figure out the right thing to do. Though far less personally challenging and threatening than the baseball phase had been, these years must have been frustrating ones.

Observers have been puzzled as well. On the one hand, Dick Young said that nothing Jackie did after baseball matched what he had done in baseball. To which Jackie angrily responded, "How could it? What could I have done?" In other words, his decade in baseball was a hard act to follow. Yet to the African American tennis star and sports historian Arthur Ashe, Jackie did more for civil rights after his playing days than during them; he was therefore "the most significant former athlete in American history."

At Chock Full o'Nuts, Jackie settled into a white-collar job routine. He drove into Manhattan every day. After working mornings in his office, he visited a different group of Chock stores every afternoon. There he talked to the employees, who were mostly from poor backgrounds and struggling with large families. Theirs was a condition very familiar to him. He had made it out of such a plight; they could too. He was an example to them of how far hard work and saving money could get you. He liked the work, and he found owner William Black greatly supportive of him.

Jackie did not limit himself to the Chock job. He did a radio show. Later he did a lively column, which received a lot of attention, for the *New York Post*.

Working with a black journalist, he wrote an autobiography. In the meantime, he always managed to be at the center of controversies. He was not one to disappear quietly, as do most retired athletes. Something he said might leak to the press. Or the press, following him everywhere, asked for his opinion on various matters. He made good copy.

Though out of baseball, he remained the spokesman for black players. He complained, for example, that certain clubs still did not have any African Americans. Comments about the Milwaukee Braves, Casey Stengel, and Roy Campanella created storms of controversy. But he began to turn to more serious issues, such as race relations in America. He was becoming an activist on behalf of the growing civil rights movement.

Jackie's retirement came at a crucial period in U.S. history. In 1954 the Supreme Court ruled that segregated schooling was unconstitutional. This, together with the bus boycott in Montgomery, Alabama, in 1955, started the civil rights movement of the next decade. Race relations replaced fear of communism as the most important item on the national agenda.

The Jim Crow laws controlling every aspect of life in the South were now suddenly under siege. Begun in baseball, the war against the old racist ways had spread to other areas of American life. Jackie's almost single-handed assault on the citadel of sports segregation, his extraordinarily successful integration of baseball, had probably done more to prepare the mood for the Supreme Court ruling and the movement than any other single event. In December 1956 the National Association for the Advancement of Colored People (NAACP) accordingly gave him a medal for his contribution to black progress.

The rest of America was catching up with him and facing the proposition that all blacks be given the basic rights now available only to star athletes. These things began happening just in those last three years of Jackie's baseball career, 1954–1956, when he felt age overtake him and he was at odds with the Dodger organization. It was exciting to him to see black Americans wake up and insist on their rights, the way he had. He said that he would much rather get full citizenship for his people than be named to baseball's Hall of Fame.

Jackie was eager to be part of the drive for African-American rights and dignity. So when he started a new career in business, he also started a new career as a prominent spokesman for the civil rights movement. He had been invited to join the NAACP during his playing days but had not done so. Now he took an active part in the organization. He became one of its directors, as well as chairman of the Freedom Fund Drive.

His job was to raise money. He insisted on throwing himself into the necessary work. He studied the relevant facts and arguments to be used in speeches, and soon he was able to speak effectively himself, not just appear as a celebrity who introduced someone more eloquent or knowledgeable. With William Black's encouragement, he followed a busy schedule of making fund-raising speeches all over the country.

When on tour on behalf of the NAACP he visited
Pittsburgh, where Branch Rickey now ran the ball
club. Rickey introduced him with ringing words.
Jackie, he said, had been the right man to integrate
baseball. Jackie's controversial statements were usually correct, and blacks should learn from him how to
fight to get their rights.

The civil rights issue at that time was complicated
and had no one solution. Jackie tried various ways of
helping the movement. He traveled on long speaking
tours for the National Conference of Christians and
Jews to argue before whites the case of black suffering.
He was sent by the NAACP to persuade blacks that
they must stop pitying themselves and do more to raise
themselves up by their own bootstraps. He made fund-
raising tours for the NAACP and for Dr. King's Southern Christian Leadership Conference (SCLC). King
had visited Jackie at his home in Connecticut, and
Jackie especially got to know one of King's assistants,
the young Jesse Jackson, who was destined for bigger
things.

Jackie worked with children at the Harlem YMCA.
He wrote protest letters to the Eisenhower administration in the late 1950s over government inaction. In
1959 he joined such luminaries as Harry Belafonte and
Dr. King in a march on the White House to protest the
slow pace of school integration. A decade earlier he
had gone to Washington to testify on black people's
loyalty to America, and now he was asking America to
keep its part of the deal.

As usual, controversy followed him. Once when he

criticized some Long Island communities for opposing school desegregation, a group of citizens retaliated with a threat to boycott Chock Full o'Nuts. Jackie's boss, William Black, stood by him and invited the citizens to take their business elsewhere. Jackie called that "his proudest moment of all." There was controversy with fellow blacks as well. At one convention of the NAACP, he accused the leaders of not having done enough for the average black person. Then when the Los Angeles chapter of the Urban League (another black civil rights organization) gave an award to Walter O'Malley for his role in opening baseball to blacks, Jackie attacked his black brothers for making a big mistake.

If he found himself at odds with blacks who were too middle-class and conservative, he was not in favor either with those who were radical and militant. Though an outspoken civil rights man, Jackie was a moderate trying to make his way through the swirling currents of black nationalism, separatism, and anti-white and anti-Semitic philosophies. He wanted his children to learn to cope with an integrated society. He was not a "turn the other cheek" type by nature, but neither did he favor the aggressive violence advocated by the new young militants. It was difficult to be a moderate on anything in the 1960s.

If Jackie was in the forefront of the battle for African-American rights, he was conservative in the area of women's rights. With the youngest boy, David, in school full-time, Rachel wanted to resume her career. Jackie strongly objected. His mother had had to work and had not been available to her children because of his irresponsible father. He himself was a good husband, father, and money earner. He saw no need for his wife to work. He wanted his children to have what he himself could not have, a mother to be there when she was needed.

Rachel persisted. Money was not the issue. A career was. She wanted to be something more than the wife of Jackie Robinson. Only slowly was Jackie able to come to understand the needs of a woman and wife. Rachel enrolled at New York University to obtain a master's degree in psychiatric nursing. They went into the city together in the morning, he to Chock, she to school. Then he would pick her up for the trip home in the late afternoon.

Similar tensions arose again for a while when she finished her studies and started working. Again he had to yield. Her first job was at the Einstein Medical School of Yeshiva University in New York City. Then she became an assistant professor at Yale University School of Nursing and the director of nursing at a New Haven hospital. She was Professor Rachel Robinson, not Mrs. Jackie Robinson.

Jackie came to realize that every member of his family had to deal with the large shadow he cast as a living legend, with the heavy burden of his achievement and fame. Each member had to struggle in his or her own way to gain acceptance.

In truth, all was not well at home. As Jack, Jr., was growing up, Jackie and Rachel became acquainted with one of the problems of being celebrities. Famous people are often too busy being famous, that is, doing whatever it is they do best, to be able to spend much time with their children. Even more awkward is the comparison forever being made between father and child.

To shield himself, Jack, Jr., would not talk in school about his father's baseball job. At school he had difficulty learning how to read and write. He did not concentrate in school or bring his homework home. When he was put into a private school, the switch did not help. The problems were compounded when his sister, Sharon, seemed to side with his younger brother, David, whenever a dispute arose.

As the years passed, Jack, Jr., turned into a troublemaker in high school. He dropped out altogether for a while. Unable to communicate as father and son, Jackie and Jack, Jr., were strangers to each other. They would argue rather than talk.

Once he was out of baseball, Jackie's deep involvement in business, civil rights, and politics made him more of a traveler than before, and he saw even less of his children. How ironic that Jackie was sometimes attending meetings and events given by organizations helping troubled youngsters at the very time that his own youngster was becoming one.

Finally in his teens, Jack, Jr., ran away from home just as Jackie had to undergo major surgery. The boy seemed to be trying to put his father out of his mind. When Jackie later looked through his son's belongings for a clue as to the boy's whereabouts, he found in an old wallet a photo of himself. The father broke down and cried over this hidden sign of love and worship.

Jack, Jr., had run off to see if he could make it on his own. In the spring of 1964, he joined the U.S. Army. Vietnam was around the corner.

19

POLITICIAN
(1960-1965)

Jackie threw himself not only into the vice-presidency at Chock Full o'Nuts and the civil rights movement but also into politics. His postbaseball life consisted of a three-pronged drive to improve conditions for his people. Through politics he hoped to create a better America in which African Americans could take their rightful place. Through civil rights organizations he hoped to make blacks more clearly worthy of such a place. And through his work at Chock he would deal with individual blacks, helping them make their entry into the middle-class world. Earning money for himself could never be the chief goal of his waking hours.

Before he became interested in politics, politicians (and others) had become interested in him. In his playing days, VIPs—President Eisenhower, Vice President Richard Nixon, General Douglas MacArthur—would visit the clubhouse for the honor of being photographed with him. Once, at a reception, President Eisenhower went out of his way to cross a large room to shake Jackie's hand. Later, during the Lyndon Johnson administration in the mid-1960s, Jackie and Rachel were invited to the White House, and the president took a turn on the dance floor with Rachel.

Jackie's entry into the political arena made controversy likely, and his decisions and choices did little to avoid it. At first, in the 1960 presidential primaries, he campaigned for Senator Hubert Humphrey, the liberal Democrat with a strong civil rights record. When Senator John Kennedy beat Humphrey in the primaries, Jackie was in a dilemma. Kennedy was as little known to Jackie as to many others. The Republican nominee was Vice President Richard Nixon.

Jackie interviewed both candidates on the civil rights question. While Jackie felt a little uncomfortable about Nixon's behavior, the meeting with Kennedy went worse. Kennedy was unable to look Jackie in the eye. Also, because Kennedy came from Massachusetts, Jackie felt he knew nothing about the problems African Americans faced. Jackie was turned off.

Reluctantly, he decided to support Nixon because the vice president had been to Africa and seemed to have gained from his governmental experience some understanding of the civil rights issue. Jackie's backing of Nixon shocked many blacks and liberals. Blacks had for decades voted for the somewhat more racially liberal northern Democrats. Even Rachel argued with him. Still, Jackie actively went to work for Nixon. That conservative streak in Jackie was showing again.

During the campaign, however, Kennedy began to look better on civil rights at the same time that Nixon distanced himself from blacks, especially from Dr. King. A disillusioned Jackie was often on the verge of quitting and denouncing Nixon. He had made a mistake. But, convinced that blacks should be represented in both parties, he decided to stay put.

Kennedy won. As it turned out, Jackie came to respect the work of President Kennedy—and even more that of his brother, Attorney General Robert Kennedy—in the area of civil rights. The Kennedy brothers had their hands full dealing with what looked at the time like the beginning of a new civil war. African-American insistence on fundamental rights supported by the federal government met with massive resistance in the South. Jackie felt he had to be with his black brothers and sisters at these times of crisis. More was needed than the speeches and the fund-raising drives of recent years. In January 1963 he joined heavyweight boxer Floyd Patterson and other prominent blacks from the sports and entertainment world in going to Jackson, Mississippi. They wanted to provide moral support for the local black population in its struggle for basic rights. In May they went to Birmingham, Alabama, for the same purpose. There they found bombed homes, rumors of active Klansmen and lynch mobs, and run-ins with the local police and state troopers.

Jackie had difficulty understanding how at the very time that four black girls were killed in a church building by white bigots, white baseball fans in New York wildly cheered Willie Mays for hitting two home runs in a game. While some baseball-playing blacks in the

North were adored, blacks in the South were being driven to desperation. The contrast made no sense at all.

In 1962 Jackie first became eligible for entry into the Baseball Hall of Fame. Such an election would finish the process begun fifteen years earlier. Considering his outspokenness, he was sure he would be rejected. Yet even the sometimes hostile Dick Young sided with Jackie, who got the necessary three-fourths vote of sportswriters.

Just before that vote, he was given a testimonial dinner at New York's famous Waldorf-Astoria Hotel by Dr. Martin Luther King's SCLC as an expression of gratitude from the black community for all that Jackie had done for King's movement. Telegrams came from President Kennedy and Vice President Johnson. New York governor Nelson Rockefeller and other notables made speeches.

In July 1962 Jackie was officially entered into the Hall of Fame. Inducted with him, ironically, was pitching great Bob Feller, who had said several times in 1946–1947 that Jackie would fail to break into the majors because he could not hit. Jackie was especially proud that his mother and his surrogate father, Branch Rickey, had lived to see this day. If the dinner at the Waldorf was an acknowledgment of all he had done for African Americans, the induction was an acknowledgment of all he had done for baseball.

At the induction ceremony in Cooperstown, New York, he shared his honor on the dais with the three people who had most to do with his achievements: his mother, his wife, and his mentor, Rickey. Rickey's noble experiment had turned out well. Officials at the ceremony helped make it the happiest day of Jackie's life by not mentioning that he was the first black man to enter the Hall of Fame.

Now, with the passage of time and the benefit of hindsight, Jackie could reflect a little more deeply on the meaning of his achievement. In 1964, with the help of a writer-editor, he wrote *Baseball Has Done It*. This book traces the entry of blacks into the majors. The autobiographical portions are mixed with interviews and reminiscences by other black players.

The book has a split personality. It contains an optimistic and a pessimistic view. The optimistic side looks at the larger picture of baseball's place within American society. It tells how integration came to baseball and how it could be achieved everywhere else in society. The desegregation of baseball—quick, peaceful, and ultimately beneficial to everyone concerned—was for Jackie a model for the desegregation of American life. The method used was simple: an appeal to American ideals and to common decency; the threat of economic pressure; the use of nonviolent confrontation.

Martin Luther King commented to Don Newcombe on his sense of indebtedness to the first baseball players for blazing a trail. When the civil rights movement began, baseball was already mostly desegregated. So were the hotels it relied on. Neither mass protests nor government intervention, neither strife nor bloodshed, brought about this sweeping change in an American institution. Baseball proved that Americans "can live together in peaceful competition." Sharing the same goal of winning, the ballplayers, black and white, did everything—travel, eat, socialize—together and thought nothing of it. In 1963, 15 percent of major league players were black, including many who had been named Rookie of the Year and Most Valuable Player, and had won batting or base-stealing championships. No racial incidents were taking place. Baseball had come a long way in surprisingly little time.

Jackie wrote that America should be following the example of baseball. But when he looked at what America was in fact doing, the book turns pessimistic. Race relations in the nation were in turmoil. Jackie's book has a wartime aura about it. It reads like a collection of bulletins from the battlefield. Those were crucial days in the civil rights movement. The book appeared on the eve of the Civil Rights Acts of 1964 and 1965, which, guaranteeing the vote to blacks in the South, brought that first phase of the civil rights movement to a triumphant conclusion and began the era of the New South with its black elected officials.

Even baseball was entangled in this civil war. Jackie stressed the unfinished business: the remaining pockets of segregation, especially in lodging in some cities; the low salaries of black baseball stars; the fact that only outstanding blacks could make it; the lack of opportunity for commercial endorsements; and the absence of managerial and front-office jobs. With reference to this last point, Jackie cited his own experi-

ence long before at Pasadena Junior College as proof
that whites will play for a black man who leads, gives
signals, and decides strategy. In the same way, stars
such as Snider, Reese, and Hodges readily took advice
from Jackie. Most players will follow anyone who can
help produce a winning team. As for himself, he wrote,
"I used to have managerial ambitions. I don't now."

Jackie's foray into the world of books was matched
a year later by one into the world of TV. His greatness
was newly acknowledged in 1965 when a documentary
of his life appeared on network TV (CBS) in a series
hosted by Mike Wallace. It was especially satisfying to
be honored while he was still alive.

20

THE TURBULENT LATER SIXTIES
(1965-1971)

A major facet of Jackie's public life in his last years was his association with New York's Republican governor, Nelson Rockefeller. Jackie first met the man in 1962. He was impressed by the governor's charm. When Rockefeller spoke out in favor of the black student protests in the South, Jackie paid even more attention. Rockefeller backed words with deeds; he gave a good deal of money to Dr. King's SCLC and to the rebuilding of bombed black churches in the South.

After Jackie's disillusionment with Nixon, he was a little more careful about giving political allegiance. He was uneasy over the fact that the New York state government had no African Americans in it and he wrote a letter to the governor on that subject. The governor responded with a grateful telephone call and held a meeting with black leaders. Out of that came a reform of state government hiring procedures. Jackie was impressed by how carefully Rockefeller listened

176

and how conscientiously he carried out suggestions. He began to work for the governor.

First he was placed on the New York State Athletic Commission. Then, in 1964, when Rockefeller decided to run for president, he asked Jackie to become one of the national directors of his campaign. Jackie now rethought his career goals, as he had in 1956. He had put in seven years at Chock Full o'Nuts. He had received nice salary raises and benefits, purchased a lot of company stock, and moved onto the board of directors of the company. But here was a chance that enabled Jackie to do more for his people. He resigned from Chock Full o'Nuts and went to work for the Rockefeller campaign.

Jackie was pleased that he was not just the specialist on black affairs. He was an assistant to the governor who happened to be black. He was asked to speak on behalf of Rockefeller to groups that were integrated or even mainly white. Sometimes he was asked to introduce Rockefeller.

He made it clear that he was campaigning for Rockefeller and not for the entire Republican party and certainly not the conservative right wing of the party. In a magazine article he attacked the leader of that wing, Senator Barry Goldwater. He predicted that were Goldwater to be the nominee of the party, the party would become all white. Jackie attended the 1964 Republican National Convention as a special delegate actively working for Rockefeller. He watched with dismay as the conservatives captured the proceedings and the mainstream Republicans fell into line. He almost got into a fistfight with a delegate from Alabama.

Interviewed on network TV, he called Goldwater a bigot. Goldwater tried to meet with Jackie to bring him around, but it was too late. Jackie had joined a newly formed organization backing the Democratic nominee, Republicans for Johnson. Asked to appear on a TV show with the formidable conservative intellectual, William F. Buckley, Jr., Jackie was warned by friends that Buckley would destroy him on camera. Drawing on his sports background, Jackie decided that the best defense was to be aggressive. He began the show by charging that the Goldwater camp was filled with racists. He felt he had enraged Buckley and had him off-balance during the rest of the program.

So now Jackie was back in the Democratic camp. In spite of backing Johnson in the election, he felt uneasy about the Democratic president, who was a Southerner. When violence against blacks flared up in Selma, Alabama, Jackie was in the South making speeches attacking the Johnson administration for not doing enough to protect blacks. Johnson soon, however, worked actively for civil rights, even adopting the "We Shall Overcome" slogan, and Jackie reversed himself. Jackie had learned in baseball that once bigoted Southerners learned to appreciate a black player's ability, they made better allies than did Northerners dealing with equality only as an idea and from a distance. Johnson was a prime example of the Southern convert to civil rights who has a sincerity sometimes lacking in Northern liberals.

Despite having strayed to the Democrats in the presidential election, Jackie remained in Rockefeller's good graces. After a period of service with the nonpolitical Rockefeller Foundation, he was appointed, in February 1966, special assistant to the governor for community affairs. This post made Jackie a member of the governor's cabinet. It was a full-time political job, and it involved a financial sacrifice. Though Jackie had not been seeking such a job, he was never one to turn down an important challenge.

His task was to represent Rockefeller, working out of the governor's Fifty-fifth Street office in New York City. Jackie was one of the few people the governor could rely on to speak out boldly. Rockefeller in turn always listened to Jackie thoughtfully (or so at least it seemed) and talked frankly with him.

In Rockefeller's 1966 campaign for reelection as governor, the very conservative congressman William Miller was being considered for the post of campaign chairman. Interviewed on the radio, Jackie said that he could not work for Rockefeller if Miller came on board. There was a big uproar. At a press conference, Rockefeller supported Jackie and rebuffed the conservatives. As a result, William F. Buckley, Jr., in his newspaper column attacked Rockefeller for being a boss who gave orders to everyone in the Republican party and the New York state government except Jackie Robinson. Jackie took this as a great compliment.

The year 1968 was a bleak one for Jackie. Dr. King and Robert Kennedy, both leading fighters for civil rights, were slain. Rockefeller was unable to mount a successful presidential nomination campaign. The Republicans nominated instead Nixon and Spiro Agnew. To Jackie, this selection showed that the Republican party had turned its back on African Americans. He therefore resigned as Rockefeller's special assistant in order to be free to campaign for the Democratic candidate, Vice President Hubert Humphrey.

It was his sixth change in party allegiance. Despite his radicalism in baseball matters and his conservatism in family matters, Jackie was trying to stake out a moderate, middle-of-the-road position in politics. He preferred to judge the politician and his program rather than the party affiliation. But as American politics is mainly a matter of working within the two-party system, one cannot blame political observers for coming to regard Jackie as indecisive, naive, and just plain foolish.

Humphrey lost to Nixon, whose administration proved to be indifferent to blacks. In presidential politics, Jackie had precious little to show for his efforts, but he could find satisfaction in his two years of work with Governor Rockefeller. He had eased the way for the appointment of qualified blacks in state government. When unrest arose in the black ghetto, he had been sent to listen and learn what ignited the trouble. He had transmitted the complaints of the militants to the higher officials in state government. He felt, in short, that his being there had made a difference.

He still tried to make a difference in baseball despite his remoteness from it. In a radio interview in

April 1969, he attacked Lee MacPhail, now a baseball executive, for saying that blacks could make it on the field but not in the front office. When MacPhail did not answer to Jackie's satisfaction, Jackie turned down an invitation to attend the old-timers day at Yankee Stadium and be honored as among "the greatest ever" according to a fan poll. Until blacks were in managerial and front-office positions, he would boycott such events.

Despite these activist gestures, Jackie's intermittent Republicanism not only surprised white liberals but also led to even more severe criticism from some blacks. A new generation of young militants arose for whom the breakthrough of the late 1940s and early 1950s was ancient history. They wanted sweeping changes, and they wanted them at once.

Jackie believed in working through the system. That had been his experience. He had turned the other cheek (at least in the first three years), he had persisted, and the establishment had yielded. The militants wanted to overturn the establishment. One slogan was "Burn, baby, burn!" To such firebrands, Jackie seemed old-fashioned. They noted that he had always been dependent on the paternalism of a white godfather—Rickey in baseball, Black in business, Rockefeller in politics. That was proof that he had not raised himself up by his bootstraps but was a puppet of some white "massa" or boss with an agenda of his own. Jackie Robinson, the destroyer of segregation in baseball and the alleged hotheaded loudmouth, was being attacked as an Uncle Tom working with and for the

181

white establishment. No wonder Jackie felt that he was still the same but the world around him had changed.

In the face of such insults, he remained open-minded. Those black militants who put Jackie down knew little of his ordeals, but he understood all too well their intense feelings. When the militant Black Panthers came along, he went to Brooklyn to meet with them. He needed to find out what they really wanted and not what the media said about them. When the media showed African-American students at Cornell University brandishing rifles, he wrote the students to find out their side of the story.

Jackie was still a fighter. In 1967, during a power struggle within the NAACP between the autocratic old-line leadership and some younger rebels, Jackie sided with the rebels. He attacked the head of the organization for being out of touch with the current mood in the black ghetto and not listening to the younger, angrier voices. The irony was that this action did not help to endear him to the youthful militants. His connections with the business community, white and black, with Republicans and with Rockefeller, no less than his commitment to nonviolence, made him suspect in their eyes.

Complicating the generational conflict was the Vietnam War. In 1965 America increased its involvement in the struggle in South Vietnam against the North Vietnamese communists. The country was torn by debate over the merits of this war. Jackie, like most Americans, at first supported our struggle in Southeast Asia. As the years passed, however, and no progress was evident, Americans started to turn against the war in growing numbers.

Blacks had their own version of dissent. The great heavyweight boxing champion Muhammad Ali refused to serve in the army on the grounds that no Vietnamese communist had ever called him "nigger." More important, Dr. King came out against the war in April 1967. To Jackie, all this must have brought back haunting memories of twenty years before. Could Paul Robeson have been right after all in 1949 in saying that blacks would not fight for America against communism?

King's stand was especially painful for Jackie. Jackie had first met him soon after the bombing of the King home in early 1956, and they had become friends. Despite his three years of turning the other cheek, Jackie did not entirely share King's philosophy of non-violence as a response to violent attacks. But Jackie respected the leader and joined King whenever his schedule permitted. King made Jackie head of the drive to raise funds to rebuild the burned-out black churches in Georgia, and it was at King's request that he had gone with Floyd Patterson to Mississippi and Alabama. But now the Vietnam War came between them.

In May 1967 Jackie wrote in his column that King was the greatest civil rights leader in history but that he was wrong to come out against the Vietnam War. King phoned Jackie, and they had a long conversation over the rift between them. It ended with Jackie gaining some understanding of and heightened respect for

King's position. Each man had a clear-cut principle. To King, violence was evil whether it took place in Alabama or in Vietnam. To Jackie, marrying the civil rights movement to the antiwar movement was a disastrous strategy for African Americans.

By the late 1960s, with increasing turbulence over black militancy, antiwar protests, and radicalism, Jackie had become a quaint and old-fashioned figure. He was drowned out by the new voices and the new issues, displaced by the new leaders. He even had tensions with his own children, who were part of the younger generation. He had to learn to listen to their kind of anger. Talking to them gave him doubts about the Vietnam War. He needed to look no further than his own family to see the awful impact of the war on America.

Jack, Jr., had joined the army in 1964. A year later he was sent to the front in Vietnam. He was wounded there. Worse, he also became addicted to drugs and involved in the Far Eastern drug underworld. He was discharged from the army in June 1967 and returned home more confused than ever. His family never suspected that he had picked up a drug addiction in the army. Then on March 6, 1968, Jackie received word that his son had been arrested in a cheap hotel for possession of marijuana, heroin, and a gun. Jackie was long used to facing reporters but never on such painful family matters.

Arrested again in August, Jack, Jr., avoided jail only by turning himself in for treatment. Jackie placed his son in a hospital, but it did no good. Jack, Jr., was then sent to Daytop, a drug rehabilitation center, where discipline was strict. Jackie and Rachel were told that if Jack, Jr., came asking to be allowed back home, they had to turn him down.

After a year filled with many difficult hours for son and parents, Jack, Jr., was cured. Partly out of gratitude and partly to remain cured, Jack, Jr., decided to join Daytop's staff and help others overcome addiction. One of his duties was to speak to individuals and groups and tell them of his addiction to the whole range of drugs—cocaine, heroin, LSD, amphetamines, even cough syrup. He had to tell about how the expenses of addiction had driven him into a nightmare world of stealing, housebreaking, pushing drugs, and pimping. He became a compelling speaker on the subject.

One day Jackie and Rachel decided to give a picnic for all the members of the Daytop staff. After the picnic, the guests got in line to individually thank the hosts. When it was Jack, Jr.'s turn, Jackie remembered that his son, when leaving for the army, had refused to hug his father because it was unmanly. So now Jackie merely put his hand out to his son. To his surprise, Jack, Jr., pushed the hand aside and hugged his father warmly. If Jack, Jr., had tried to put his father out of his mind by using drugs, Daytop had helped the son find his father by putting drugs out of his mind.

Jackie was moved as never before. His own prodigal son was back. The family was close again. Years of alienation and misunderstanding and pain were finished.

During his seven years at Chock Full o'Nuts, Jackie had become acquainted with the world of finance. Now he thought he could use this knowledge and the business connections he had made. He decided to start his own business. He hoped other African Americans would do so too. He continued to believe that blacks could advance themselves not by pleading for charity but by self-reliance. They had to use the power of the vote and of the dollar.

He was therefore interested when a black businessman in Harlem approached him about starting a bank. The bank would be owned and run by and for black people. Blacks needed their own bank because they had problems obtaining loans for houses, businesses, or cars from the regular banks. White bankers often assumed, out of prejudice or ignorance, that blacks could not be relied on to repay the money they borrowed. This new bank, to be called the Freedom National Bank, would make it easier for African Americans to get loans. Jackie became chairman of the board.

The venture proved to be a headache. First there was a bitter falling-out with the man who had brought him in and who was giving himself a large expense account. A replacement was picked to handle the day-to-day running of the bank. He turned out to be incompetent. The bank had lowered standards too much in making loans, and many of them ended up being written off as losses. The result was a conflict on the board of directors of the bank between Jackie's men and the bank president's men. Only with difficulty could the bank be turned back on course.

There were other business ventures. Jackie was excited about participating in a black-owned and -run company that would build houses for low-income families. He also had an interest in a black insurance company that would, like the Freedom National Bank, fill a void left by the regular, white-run companies. In addition, he became vice president of Sea Host, a food-franchising company that tried to establish branches all over the world.

When the Senate Business Committee was looking into the franchise business, Jackie testified in January 1970 before the committee. He attacked President Nixon for having reneged on his pledge to promote black capitalism. His main point was that "making more black millionaires is not as important as moving people from $6,000 a year to $15,000."

He had come to regret ever having backed Nixon in 1960. In February 1970 Jackie wrote the president to complain that he surrounded himself with men hostile to African-American aspirations and hopes. Nixon's reply was vague but seemed to Jackie to open a door ("I enlist your help."). Jackie wrote back offering to help in any way, but nothing came of it. The door to national politics remained closed to Jackie.

21

THE BITTER END
(1971-1972)

Jackie's body was malfunctioning. He was found to have diabetes, a disease of uncontrolled blood sugar levels that affected his circulation and probably caused his difficulties with knees and feet during the last playing years. Already, while working at Chock, at the age of only forty, he had had to use a cane. In the mid-1960s he had to have a serious operation. Right after the operation, he came down with a staph infection. His condition worsened.

At this time Branch Rickey was also ailing, but he took the trouble to come to New York to see Jackie. Their warm relationship, now nearly twenty years old, had made history. They could look back with pride at the revolution they had accomplished.

Then in December 1965, Rickey died. Jackie was deeply moved. This father-son relationship had actually deepened after Jackie left baseball. It no longer had any business aspects and had become entirely personal. Rickey, always concerned to hear how Jackie was doing, followed Jackie's vigorous role in the civil rights movement with enthusiasm.

Jackie was grieved that few black players attended Rickey's funeral. Many blacks would not be where they were had it not been for him. Yet they did not even bother to send flowers or telegrams. The new generation of ballplayers had forgotten the pioneer of a generation earlier who made it possible for them to play.

Three years later an even greater loss overtook Jackie. In May 1968 he received word that his mother was dying. By the time he flew to Pasadena, she was gone. It had been a special joy for him to have been able to repay her for her years of sacrifice. He had fulfilled his boyhood dream of providing her with a decent home, a garden, and a nest egg in the bank. She had also been present in Cooperstown when her son, inducted into the Hall of Fame, gave much of the credit to her. All those years of anxiety and struggle had borne fruit. She could hardly have had a better ending to her difficult life.

Three years later came the cruelest blow of all. On June 17, 1971, Jack, Jr., died in an auto accident in Connecticut at the age of twenty-four. Bad as the death of one's child is, it was made even worse by the realization that Jack, Jr., was making a tremendous comeback. At the time of his death, he had been off drugs for three years. He had become an inspiration to others who had similar problems. He had not only saved himself but was helping save others. In fact, he was in the midst of his biggest project, lining up musicians for a benefit concert to raise money for Daytop.

Jackie Robinson

In the past, when the Robinson home was the scene of a charity social, Rachel and her friends had handled the arrangements. This time, Jack, Jr., alone was in charge, the first time he had such responsibilities. Working day and night, he was doing an excellent job with it. In the middle of all this came the car crash.

When Jackie got the word, he went into shock. He could not bring himself to go to identify the body. He was further overwhelmed by the outpouring of sympathy from people who had been helped by Jack, Jr. Being told of all that he had meant to them made the loss all the more unbearable.

Six days after the funeral, the benefit jazz concert Jack, Jr., had organized was held as scheduled. It was dedicated to his memory.

What helped Jackie survive the loss and the grief was his interest in his other two children. Daughter Sharon was at Howard University, where she insisted on keeping her family identity a secret. Receiving a degree as a nurse in 1973, she was proud to have been able to establish her worth on her own. Son David took off a year from school and went hitchhiking around the world.

The psychological blow of the death of a son must have taken its terrible toll on a body already racked with diabetes and high blood pressure and heart trouble. In April 1972 Gil Hodges suddenly died of a heart attack. When Jackie attended the funeral in Brooklyn he could hardly walk. His sight was so poor that he

190

did not notice Pee Wee Reese sitting nearby. Onlookers could not believe that this was Jackie Robinson.

When Roger Kahn's book, *The Boys of Summer*—on the Dodgers in 1952–1953 and in 1970—hit the best-seller list in the summer of 1972, it led to a new interest in Jackie, and he began to receive a lot of letters. Blind in one eye, with blurry vision in the other, he could not read the letters and, more painful for a chronic letter writer, could not answer most of them. As news of his diabetes-related eye trouble circulated, a black woman in Detroit telegrammed to offer one of her own eyes to him. Such a deeply moving example of his importance in the lives of others made him more determined to continue to live productively.

That is why, despite his ill health, he kept on traveling across the country giving speeches. He urged the baseball world to open more doors for blacks, especially in front-office positions. He was active in other ways. Baseball player Curt Flood had refused to allow himself to be traded without his permission and had brought legal suit in a case which was to lead to greater freedom and larger salaries for players. During the court proceedings, Jackie unexpectedly showed up.

He walked slowly and with difficulty into the court and sat down near a surprised Flood. He had volunteered to take the stand and testify on the difficulties of being a ballplayer, on the many advantages that the owners had over the players. Jackie was one of the few former players willing to testify for Flood about a problem they all faced. Though he was prosperous now and remote from baseball, he would not forget what he had been up against and with what the young players still had to contend.

Jackie also kept pace with new approaches within the black community to help fellow blacks. He came to know well the dynamic Reverend Jesse Jackson. He was a guest at Jackson's home in Chicago. He was a guest speaker at the Saturday morning meetings of Jackson's organization and was impressed by Jackson's dedication to helping people. When, in early 1972, Jackson resigned from the SCLC and founded People United to Save Humanity (PUSH), Jackie was proud to become first vice president. The thirty-one-year-old protégé of Dr. King seemed to Jackie to offer great and rare leadership to African Americans and other minorities.

In 1972 Jackie published yet another autobiography, *I Never Had It Made*. If his 1964 book shows a conflict between the optimist and the pessimist, in this book pessimism triumphs. He expresses deep disillusionment with baseball and with America. Writing the foreword to his book in his comfortable home in Stamford, as a successful, prosperous, and fulfilled man, he feels unable to salute the flag of the country that made his success possible. He feels he is a black man in a white world, as much now as in 1947 or 1919. His life had been shaped by his skin color. He sounds eerily like the Paul Robeson he had once attacked. About that, he writes, "In those days I had much more faith in the ultimate justice of the American white man than I have today. I would reject such an invitation [to testify] if offered now." He had now a better under-standing of the issues. He had come to respect Robeson as a man who sacrificed himself and his career for his people.

He changed his mind also about Dr. King's ideas. Though he once opposed King's anti–Vietnam War stand, he was no longer sure that King was wrong in 1967. Jackie had become cynical about America's role in Vietnam, especially about what the war did to the black American GI.

Why should an African American have fought for freedom in Vietnam when he himself had little of it at home? That question had been raised in World Wars I and II and in the Korean War, by Robeson, by King, and now by Jackie himself. "There was a time when I deeply believed in America. I have become bitterly disillusioned."

Jackie sounds quite radical and militant, even em-bittered. He feels that blacks are written off by the Republicans and taken for granted by the Democrats. With white people "consolidated to destroy us," blacks must develop an effective and selfish policy to protect themselves.

Even baseball, now the most democratic of sports, is sick, Jackie feels. It exploits gifted young black bod-ies and then discards them. While posing as a sacred institution dedicated to the public good, it is just big business, ruthless in ways that few businesses can match. It makes a lot of money for a few people and concerns itself only with the price of the entrance ticket. Racism is still widespread, as seen in the unwillingness of baseball to give managerial and administrative positions to blacks. As always, he is sure he would have been a good manager. And as always he has one succinct reply to his critics' claim that he was ungrateful: "Baseball and I are even. I got a lot. I gave a lot."

What a grim summing up *I Never Had It Made* is. How ironic and sad that one of the great American success stories should have so soured on America. But that was because Jackie refused to turn his face away from all those who did not make it. Though a bitter pill to white America, his disillusionment is a proof of his integrity and altruism and imagination. His complaints about the unfinished business in America were —and are—correct.

The twenty-fifth anniversary of Jackie's entry into major league baseball was celebrated in 1972. *Sport* magazine honored Jackie as the "most significant athlete" of the past quarter century. Basketball star Bill Russell said that Jackie was someone special and rare, "a man." In Chicago, Jesse Jackson's PUSH organization held a Jackie Robinson Day, a "Tribute to Black Excellence." An entire Saturday meeting of PUSH was devoted to saluting Jackie and his family.

In June of that year he attended Dodger Stadium in Los Angeles to commemorate the anniversary. It was a return to his old team and to the city near where he had grown up. His number, 42, was retired. His hesitant walk and his poor eyesight shocked everyone. He could not even recognize Roy Campanella.

As part of the continuing observance of the anniversary, Commissioner Bowie Kuhn invited Jackie to throw out the ball at the second game of the World Series. On October 15, before the start of the game, Red Barber, himself retired, introduced Jackie on the field. Jackie gave a brief talk, thanking his family, teammates, and fans. That was the usual stuff from ballplayers on such occasions.

But then came words that were usual for Jackie and for no one else. He once again urged baseball to hire black managers and third-base coaches. Someone afterward asked Jackie why he would want to embarrass baseball before the huge TV audience. Jackie replied that that was precisely why he did do it—what better time and place? He remained incorrigible, a fighter for justice, an unashamed and shameless teller of uncomfortable truths to the very end.

His determination was all the more impressive given the lack of attention and appreciation it received. After the ceremonies, Jackie was taken to the dressing room of the Oakland Athletics, where the black players were expected to express their admiration for what he had done. Unfortunately the players there took little interest in him.

A growing pessimism seemed to envelop him in his final months. Although he felt that life had been very good to him, he still believed that he "never had it made." He had won trophies and awards, established a great record in baseball, had a financial shelter, a comfortable home, a loving family. He had had the chance to serve others and to work with and talk to some of the most influential people in the country. But just because he had been lucky he could not forget the unlucky ones. So many of his black brothers and sisters were still living in poverty and suffering and oppression, while America seemed to be sinking deeper into racism. He felt alienated both from baseball and from America.

On October 23, 1972, Jackie returned home from a speaking engagement for Governor Rockefeller in Albany, New York. With sight weakened by chronic bleeding behind the eyes, he was working on another speech when he collapsed. It was his second heart attack. He was rushed to the hospital. On the next day, Tuesday, October 24, 1972, Jackie Robinson died.

The funeral was on October 27. Present were black baseball stars, Joe Louis, Governor Rockefeller, and a large delegation from President Nixon. Rachel asked the Reverend Jesse Jackson to give the eulogy. In his remarks, Jackson noted the direct link between Jackie's accomplishments on the baseball field and the landmark 1954 Supreme Court ruling on desegregation. He summarized Jackie's life and career in one perfect short sentence: "He turned a stumbling block into a stepping-stone."

The hearse moved through Harlem and through Bedford-Stuyvesant as many thousands lined the streets. Jackie was buried a few miles from where Ebbets Field used to be.

Jackie represents a gigantic step in the evolution from slavery to real freedom and equality. Between slavery and freedom lay almost a century of segregation, and Jackie Robinson and Branch Rickey helped end that phase. If America was ever to be an integrated society, its national pastime proved to be the one institution where the long, complex process could begin in the least painful and in the speediest fashion.

That is only half the story. A good number of sports experts consider Jackie one of the greatest, if not the greatest, all-around American athletes. That means that if he had been white and had had no role at all in the civil rights movement, he still would have left an indelible mark in the history of American sports. So he was someone special in two different ways—as a supreme athlete and as a man of rare courage fighting for a noble cause.

A Canadian newspaper put it well: "Because there was a Jackie Robinson, future generations have forgotten there was ever a need for a Jackie Robinson." Branch Rickey believed that no other black man "could have done what he did in those first two or three years." Only Jackie had the outstanding intelligence and guts that were necessary. "Surely God was with me when I picked Jackie."

FURTHER READING

There is a great need for a comprehensive scholarly biography of this major historical figure and authentic American hero. For now, the following books are useful.

Allen, Maury. *Jackie Robinson*. New York: Franklin Watts, 1987. Sketchy as a biography but, like the Golenbock book, enlivened by interviews, in this case not with fans but with people who dealt with Jackie, mostly relatives and ballplayers.

Barber, Red. *1947: When All Hell Broke Loose in Baseball*. Garden City, N.Y.: Doubleday, 1982. A delightful recounting of everything that happened in baseball during the year of Jackie's breaking into the majors, written by one of the sages and poets of the sport.

Frommer, Harvey. *Rickey and Robinson*. New York: Macmillan, 1982. Short, quick-paced version of their lives and of the history they made at their intersection.

Golenbock, Peter. *Bums: An Oral History of the Brooklyn Dodgers*. New York: Doubleday, 1984. A very colorful rendition of what the modern Dodgers meant to a multiethnic generation growing up in Brooklyn. Racy interviews with representative individuals.

Kahn, Roger. *The Boys of Summer*. New York: New American Library, 1971. Jackie seen in the context of the great Dodgers covered by the author as a reporter in 1952–1953 and then revisited nearly two decades later.

Further Reading

Robinson, Jackie, with Charles Dexter. *Baseball Has Done It*. Philadelphia: J.B. Lippincott, 1964. Autobiographical sketches intermingled with reminiscences by black players on breaking into the major leagues. A sort of owner's manual for the civil rights movement.

———, with Alfred Duckett. *I Never Had It Made*. New York: G.P. Putnam's Sons, 1972. The first half is a quick-paced recapitulation of the by-now well-recorded early life and athletic career. The second half tells of the lesser-known Jackie, the life he led after baseball. This section is informative even though there is a tendency to settle scores and to be defensive about his role in certain controversies.

Rowan, Carl T., with Jackie Robinson. *Wait Till Next Year: The Life of Jackie Robinson*. New York: Random House, 1960. Somewhat dated and long-winded, this book remains a source for much information about Jackie's early life and baseball days.

Tygiel, Jules. *Baseball's Great Experiment: Jackie Robinson and His Legacy*. New York: Oxford University Press, 1983. A scholarly and definitive study of the integration of major league baseball.

INDEX

Index

Index